The
Secret
of the
Stairs

The
Secret
of the
Stairs

Wade E. Taylor

A Guide to Spiritual Growth
from the Song of Solomon

WADE TAYLOR PUBLICATIONS
www.wadetaylorpublications.org

The Secret of the Stairs

Sixth Edition
Revised and Enlarged
First Printing September 2003
Second Printing This Edition 2009

ISBN 0-9747690-3-7

Scripture quotations are from the *King James Easy Reading Study Bible*, unless otherwise indicated. Copyright 2002 © G.E.M. Publishing.

In the *King James Easy Reading Study Bible*, archaic forms are replaced with current usage. Otherwise, it is a word for word rendering of the King James text.

Scripture quotations marked ASV are taken from the *American Standard Version* of the Bible and those marked NAS are taken from the *New American Standard Bible*; Copyright © by The Lockman Foundation; used by permission.

Scripture words shown in "*italics*" are not in the original text, but are added by translators to make the passage mean what they think it should mean. In most cases, it is best to either delete or ignore the words in italics.

At times, comments are added by Wade Taylor within Scripture references. These comments are enclosed within parentheses, and are not meant to change or add to the Word of God, but rather to clarify or emphasize what the author is saying.

CONTENTS

FOREWORD

The Story Behind The Secret of the Stairs

In 1957, Wade Taylor received a very special revelation of the message within the Song of Solomon. As a Bible school student, he had driven a group of fellow students to an outstation in New Jersey. Saturday evening, hoping that they would get together to pray about the meetings on Sunday, he was disappointed when the others decided to watch television instead.

Feeling a stirring in his spirit, he excused himself and went to his room, randomly opening his Bible to the Song of Solomon. As he began to read, something very unusual happened; he became a part of the Song of Solomon, and the Lord enacted within him the lives of each of the three main characters, Solomon, the Bride, and the Daughters of Jerusalem.

The Lord allowed Wade Taylor to experience, one by one, the progression of events within the Song of Solomon, from the perspective of each of the participants, feeling as they felt and thinking the thoughts that they thought.

This profound experience lasted several hours. When the Spirit of the Lord lifted, Wade realized that a deeper understanding of the Song of Solomon, with a new and fresh perspective, had been imparted to him.

The Lord had *"opened"* to him the message within the Song of Solomon as being a manual on spiritual growth, as well as a description of the processes used to bring into spiritual maturity all those who hunger to better know the Lord, and become His Bride.

As this took place, Wade thought, *"Now I have something to speak, as now I have this understanding."* But the Lord rebuked him and said: *"You are not to speak it! Rather, you are to live it. And in time, you are to teach the experience of it."*

It was not until 1970 when Wade spoke at a small conference in Virginia Beach that he felt released to share what the Lord had revealed to him, years earlier. The reel-to-reel tapes from these messages were transcribed by his son, William Taylor. In 1976, the edited transcripts were published as a 53-page booklet called, *The Secret of the Stairs*, with a press run of 2,000, which was reprinted several more times.

In 1987, it was expanded into a 157-page book. Since then it has been enlarged twice and reprinted a number of times. The latest, the 5th edition, was expanded to 185 pages, making it easier to read and understand.

Now, in 2009, it is again enlarged to make the message it contains yet more readable and understandable.

INTRODUCTION

The message in this book, *The Secret of the Stairs*, is directed toward those who actively desire to come into the fullness of all that our Lord desires for them, those who are spiritually hungry and identify with the heart cry of the Apostle Paul:

"That I may know Him....." Philippians 3:10

As the message within *The Secret of the Stairs* becomes a personal reality within us, we, together with the Bride, will be able to say:

"My Beloved *is* **white and ruddy, the chiefest among ten thousand. His head** *is as* **the most fine gold, His locks** *are* **bushy,** *and* **black as a raven. His eyes** *are* **as** *the eyes* **of doves by the rivers of waters, washed with milk,** *and* **fitly set. His cheeks** *are* **as a bed of spices,** *as* **sweet flowers: His lips** *like* **lilies, dropping sweet smelling myrrh. His hands** *are as* **gold rings set with the beryl: His belly** *is as* **bright ivory overlaid** *with* **sapphires. His legs** *are as* **pillars of marble, set upon sockets of fine gold: His countenance** *is* **as Lebanon, excellent as the cedars. His mouth** *is* **most sweet: yea, He** *is* **altogether lovely. This** *is* **my Beloved, and this** *is* **my Friend, O Daughters of Jerusalem."** Song of Solomon 5:10-16

The Song of Solomon sets forth the development of a beautiful love relationship between our Heavenly Bridegroom and His Bride in such expressive imagery, that we are enlightened, challenged, and drawn closer to Him. It not only reveals the desire of the Lord to draw us into quality times of intimate communion and ministry *with* Him, but also presents the method and means by which this can be accomplished.

This applies to those who have fully consecrated their lives to the Lord and have "*touched*" Him in some measure, yet still have a burning desire to *better* know Him, and also, to grow into an intimate relationship with Him.

We may have a wonderful testimony: "*The Lord told me to go... or, the Lord said to do...*" but, there is something beyond all *spiritual activity*, which our Lord greatly desires. This was shown to me in a special way when the Lord quickened me concerning what I considered to be a calling to Uruguay in South America. As I prayerfully held this before the Lord, I felt that I had completely consecrated my life on this point. I was willing to go and waited only for the Lord's confirmation.

I said, "*Lord, why don't You speak and tell me, then I will know what to do?*" A short time later, the Lord unfolded the following understanding to me through a very clear impression within my spirit.

"*If I speak and tell you to go, it will destroy the very thing I desire to accomplish within your life. If I were to continually speak to you and say "go" here or there, or "do" this or that, our relationship would become like that of an employer and employee. When an employer tells his employee, 'I want you to do thus and so,' the employee responds, 'Yes, sir, I will do it.' Then, at the end of the week, after he has done all these things, he returns to his employer with his hand out, saying, 'I have done all that you required of me; now I am ready for my paycheck.'*"

After I saw this, the Lord clearly said: "*I desire our relationship to be as an intimate love relationship, that of a Bridegroom with His Bride, rather than that of an employer and employee.*" He is our head; we are the members of His body. Therefore, we are to flow together with Him, as being "*one.*" Jesus prayed for this *oneness* in our relationship to Him.

"That they all may be one; as You, Father, *are* in Me, and I in You, that they also may be one in Us: that the world may believe that You have sent Me." John 17:21

We are to become *one* with Him in intent and in experience, even as Jesus exhibited, or manifested the Father on earth. Jesus said, "*He that has seen Me has seen the Father*" (John 14:9). He was saying, "*I so perfectly do the will of My Father, and I am so completely in accord with Him, that all I say or do is exactly as He would have said or done, which reflects Him. Therefore, if you have seen Me, you have seen Him.*"

Jesus said, "*You shall be witnesses*" (Acts 1:8). This means that I am to come into such intimate unity with my Lord that my life will reflect, or set forth in open view, His nature and character. My life should witness to, or reveal Jesus in such completion and fullness that I will be able to say, as the Apostle Paul said:

"Be you followers of me, even as I also *am* of Christ." I Corinthians 11:1

This is what the Lord meant when He said to me, "*I do not intend our relationship to be that of an employer and an employee. Instead, it is to be as a marriage relationship in which there is such oneness and unity, that I will be able to reveal Myself through you.*"

Paul said in Galatians 2:20, "*I am crucified with Christ.*" This word, "*crucified,*" expresses the fact that the "*I*" has been put to death. In the beginning there was only one will, the will of God. All creation was submitted to His will and resounded to the Glory of God in harmony and obedience. Then Satan rose up and said, "*I will ascend... I will be like the most High*" (Isaiah 14:13-14). Now, there were two wills: "*Thy will*" and "*I will.*"

These two wills *crossed*; that is, they were contrary, one to the other, forming a cross in heaven before there ever was one on earth. Then Satan caused sin to enter the Garden of Eden. Now, these two conflicting wills adversely affected the earth, and the man whom God had created. Jesus came and died on this cross, paying the full penalty for the resultant sin, and made it possible for us to again choose *"Thy will,"* and function with Him in harmony and submissive obedience. Jesus said:

"If any *man* **will come after Me, let him deny himself, and take up his cross, and follow Me."** Matthew 16:24

To take up my cross means that I must cross out my *"self-will,"* or my *"I-will."* This crucifies my-own way (*will*), and I again become one-with-Him. Thus, my will is submitted to and merged into His will. Now, His will has become my will, and I am free to follow Him.

When the Scripture says that we *"crucify the Son of God afresh"* (Hebrews 6:6), it means that *"my will"* has risen up against (*crossed*) the will of God. I press to have my own way, grieving and breaking the heart of the Lord. As He chastens me in love, I respond by quickly bringing *"my"* desires to the cross, for I have learned that His will for me is far better than anything I may desire for myself. Jesus died that we might become *one with Him.* He gave the Holy Spirit to abide within us that we might come forth into the victory and fullness of His Body, complete in perfect *union* and *communion* with Him.

The Lord desires to bring us into a higher level of spiritual experience in which *"our will"* is totally merged into *"His will,"* where we are no longer working *"for"* Him, but we are joined together *"with"* Him *"as one"* in a dependent, cooperative relationship.

"Who *is* **this that comes up from the wilderness, leaning upon her Beloved...?"** Song of Solomon 8:5

The desire of the Lord, as revealed in the Song of Solomon, is to make known to us the *"way,"* or the method of entrance to the *stairs*, which will lead us upward into His chambers. As we partake of the message within this book, *The Secret of the Stairs*, we will progress ever upward upon these stairs, that we might come into this experience of union and communion with our Heavenly Bridegroom.

The Lord seeks a Bride who is willing to yield her (*self*) identity and the totality of her being, that she might come into a life of complete *submission* to, and *union* with her Heavenly Bridegroom.

"My Beloved spoke, and said to me, Rise up, My love, My fair one, and come away." Song of Solomon 2:10

This is a call to respond to the processes of God, which progressively unfold within the lives of those who seek to know Him more fully and personally.

The principles that are revealed within this book will guide us from our new birth experience to spiritual maturity. As we personally respond to His desire for a Bride, this book will become a priceless guide that will lead us to the Bridegroom who waits for us, within His chambers.

The spiritual truths which are hidden within the Song of Solomon can be extracted and understood only through a developing love relationship with Jesus Himself. Those who approach this book intellectually will never be able to plumb the depths of the truths it contains. As we seek to better know the Lord, we must learn to listen to Him in our spirit, rather than through our mind. There is a spiritual *"listening"* which can be cultivated within those who are redeemed. Jesus said:

"Who has ears to hear, let him hear." Matthew 13:9

He is not speaking about our physical ability to hear. We are in essence spiritual beings, and within each of us is an inner ear, the ear of our spirit, through which *"we hear spiritually."*

As we listen to Him with this inner spiritual ear, truth is deposited in our spirit. It may take days, months, or even years for the Lord to organize the circumstances of our lives in such a way that this truth can be released to move from the innermost depths of our being, up into our consciousness.

We tend to reverse this process by approaching spiritual truth with our intellect, thinking that all this will simultaneously be received into our spirit.

Spiritual truth always moves "*upward.*" Therefore, *when anointed,* truth is imparted within our spirit, into the inner depths of our being, and then gradually works its way up into the realm of our physical mind and understanding. As we patiently hold our spirit before the Lord, a process of *spiritual transfer* takes place, resulting in the Lord being able to more fully reveal Himself to us, satisfying our spiritual hunger and desire for Him.

To better receive the rich deposit of spiritual truth that is hidden within the *Song of Solomon,* we should, with heart sincerity, give expression to the following prayer as we begin to read *The Secret of the Stairs.*

"Lord, I ask You to enlarge my spiritual hunger and capacity. Anoint and guide me as I begin to partake of the Song of Solomon. Release me from every hindrance, that I might begin to move into the spiritual reality that You have waiting for me within its pages."

"I love You Lord, and I trust You with my life. Without qualification, I totally place myself in Your hands that You might *work* the message of this book into the fiber of my being. Create within me the capacity to understand the spiritual principles contained in this book."

"Lord, I ask that these truths become personalized within me. Only then will I be changed, and others helped through my experience.

Only You can make of me the Bride that You desire, as You have revealed throughout the Song of Solomon. I ask that You move into my life, to cause me to become this Bride that You so longingly desire."

"Lord, as I read, speak to me, and work within me. Thank You, Lord Jesus. Amen."

Let us begin this journey toward intimacy with Jesus in His chambers. As we enter, we will find the satisfaction that we have longed for, and for which we were created.

Chapter 1

DRAW ME

"The song of songs, which *is* Solomon's."
Song of Solomon 1:1

The message within the Song of Solomon develops around a Bridegroom who is actively seeking a Bride from *among* the Daughters of Jerusalem. In order to understand the message of this book and receive the value that it has for us, we must prayerfully read ourselves into the progressive action that unfolds within its pages.

This *"Bridegroom"* is our Lord Jesus Christ. He is still seeking after and preparing a Bride – those *within* the Church who have a single eye toward Him and are seeking to intimately know Him. The Song of Solomon is invaluable to those who desire to have a part in the coming *"marriage supper of the Lamb."*

"And he says to me, Write, Blessed *are* they which are called to the marriage supper of the Lamb. And he says to me, These are the true sayings of God."
Revelation 19:9

The Lord greatly desires that we choose Him above all else, that we might become a part of this corporate *"Bride"* that He is yet apprehending, and with whom He desires to be fully united. As we progressively respond to Him, He will patiently, yet determinedly, draw us step upon step, *ever upward*, toward His chambers. Here, in the intimacy of His

17

presence, we become *"one"* as we partake with Him in intimate fellowship, and then participate with Him in the outworking of His purposes.

The *"Daughters of Jerusalem"* depict the many Christians who view and relate to the Bridegroom in a different (*lesser*) realm than His Bride. Although these Daughters will not be called to the coming *"marriage supper of the Lamb,"* they continually affect the developing relationship between the Bride and the Bridegroom.

As we prayerfully compare our personal desires and goals to those of the Bride, and then, in contrast to those of the Daughters of Jerusalem, we will gain much understanding concerning our spiritual condition and the corrections that we should make. Also, we will be challenged, as was the Apostle Paul, to *"press toward the mark for the prize of the high calling of God in Christ Jesus"* (Philippians 3:14); for there is far more available to us than just maintaining our salvation and waiting for heaven.

We will benefit most from the Song of Solomon by comparing *our* attitudes and responses to the Lord, with those of the Bride to the Bridegroom. As the hindrances to her relationship with the Bridegroom unfold before us, we should begin to recognize similar problems that deter our spiritual growth. Then, we will be able to make the changes that she makes in order to become *"one"* with Him.

We must *"qualify"* and be *"chosen"* by Him to become His Bride.

"For many are called, but few *are* chosen." Matthew 22:14

All this begins with the expression of the Bride's heart desire toward the Bridegroom:

"Draw me, we will run after You....." Song of Solomon 1:4

And the result:

"...the King has brought me into His chambers...."
Song of Solomon 1:4

This prayer of desire, and the declaration of the Bride's willingness to respond to any steps that He might take toward her, turned the heart of the Bridegroom singularly toward her, and set the stage for all that follows in the development of their relationship, as seen progressively within the Song of Solomon.

The first part is an extremely important prayer, consisting of only two words:

"Draw me."

Next, she makes a firm commitment to the Bridegroom:

"We will run after You."

The third part is the glorious result of her desire and consecration:

"The King has brought me into His chambers."

This essential prayer, *"Draw me,"* relates to our spiritual hunger. Hunger is basic to all life and finds its satisfaction in many forms. Our spiritual hunger is a part of this. It must overcome and rise above all of the natural *"urges of life"* that are deep within us and motivate our actions in relation to our self-life. As we lift our desire for the Lord above all other desires, and determine that He, and He alone, will feed and satisfy this hunger, we, *as overcomers*, will be ready to be brought into His chambers.

We must pray to *personally* experience this intense spiritual hunger and desire for the Lord. In the physical realm, a baby is born hungry. The mother does not create the child's hunger; she simply satisfies it. Spiritual hunger cannot be created by man. It is the result of a creative act of God and comes only from Him. This is why the Bride cried out, *"Draw me."* At the beginning of their relationship, she wanted her desire for Him to be enlarged.

A primary means to accomplish this is to present ourselves before the Lord, and then actively *"wait upon Him"* by quietly holding ourselves before Him, so this spiritual hunger can be created and activated within us. As this hunger begins to manifest itself and we cry out for its satisfaction, the Lord will respond in anticipation of making Himself known to us.

> **"And to one He gave five talents, to another two, and to another one; to every man according to his several ability; and immediately took His journey."** Matthew 25:15

These *"talents"* relate to our spiritual capacity. Once we become spiritually hungry, we must be careful to separate our newly acquired spiritual hunger from all other desires, and not allow some substitute to *seemingly* satisfy it. Nor should we seek some other means than the Lord Himself to satisfy our spiritual hunger.

As we actively look to the Lord and prayerfully ask Him to *"draw us,"* this hunger within us will *intensify,* causing us to cry out for its satisfaction. The Lord will respond and come to *"sup"* with us. As we welcome His presence and begin to *"feed Him"* with our worship, and with the expression of our commitment to *"run after Him,"* He in turn, will *"feed us,"* fully satisfying our hunger with Himself.

> **"For My flesh is meat indeed, and My blood is drink indeed. He that eats My flesh, and drinks My blood, dwells in Me, and I in him. As the living Father has sent Me, and I live by the Father: so he that eats Me, even he shall live by Me."** John 6:55-57

Our Lord is a seeking God, who is both desirous and anxious for our fellowship. He will, as we seek to better know Him, *create* within us the spiritual hunger (*desire*) that will lead us into His presence to personally and intimately sup with Him.

"Behold, I stand at the door, and knock: if any man hear My voice, and open the door, I will come in to him, and will sup with him (*we feed Him*)**, and he with Me** (*He feeds us*)**."** Revelation 3:20 (comments added)

This *"dining with Jesus"* has to do with our partaking of His very life, thereby becoming a part of Him.

"For we are members of His body, of His flesh, and of His bones." Ephesians 5:30

As our spiritual hunger increases and we are spiritually stirred, we will be moved upon (*quickened*) by the Holy Spirit to wait with expectancy, before the *"door"* that leads into His chamber. Here, we must set aside all that is earthly in order to enter into the intimacy of His presence.

"Blessed is **the man that hears Me, watching daily at My gates, waiting at the posts of My doors. For whoso finds Me finds life, and shall obtain favor of the Lord."** Proverbs 8:34-35

Only as we enter into this relationship of coming to *intimately* know the Lord, will we find the completion that was intended in our original creation. The outworking of this aspect of our spiritual growth will bring us progressively closer to Him, and to the unfolding of His purposes for us.

This increased *"sensitivity"* to His presence, and our *"responsiveness"* to His desire for our fellowship, will induce our Heavenly Bridegroom to knock upon the door of our heart more often. Now, His *"approbation"* (*divine favor*) rests upon us, as He desires us with a single eye, apart from all others - as though we were the only person in the universe.

"I sleep, but my heart wakes: it is **the voice of my Beloved that knocks,** saying, **Open to Me, My sister, My love, My dove, My undefiled: for My head is filled with dew,** and **My locks with the drops of the night."** Song of Solomon 5:2

The Lord had been out in the "*night*" searching for someone who longed to be with Him. Even this limited (*I sleep*) expression of desire (*my heart wakes*) to be with Him, moved the Lord to respond.

You have a hidden garden, Lord,
Where You seek for Your own,
Bidding them come apart
and rest sweetly with You alone.

Take me into Your garden, Lord,
See! I stand at the gate;
Open wide the golden portals,
Lest I enter too late.

Lead me gently upon Your arm
Into a place apart;
Take me into Your garden,
Lord, receive me into Your heart.

Thus, *spiritual hunger* is the foundation of our fellowship and communion with the Lord, and of our growth into spiritual maturity.

Chapter 2

WE WILL RUN AFTER YOU

The next step begins with the declaration of her commitment: *"We will run after You."* The word *"we"* portrays every part of us, *our will, intellect, and emotions*, totally seeking after and responding to the Lord. Paul said:

> **"I am crucified with Christ: nevertheless I live; yet not I, but Christ lives in me....."** Galatians 2:20

We may quote this verse and even testify about it; but there is a *spiritual law* involved. Truth is never ours until we have experienced it, and it has become a part of us. Then, we also can say, *"I live, yet not I."*

We must be certain that we have *"counted the cost,"* and that we are fully determined to *"run after Jesus,"* because He will respond to this commitment. He will begin by causing the *"letter"* of His Word to become *"experientially"* a part of us. As a result, our understanding of the Word, and our spiritual experiences, will become so alive and real that we will begin to personally know and love Jesus as never before.

The Lord will arrange all of the necessary circumstances to make this possible. We must be careful to recognize that there is a *spiritual purpose and value* in all that we experience in our daily pattern of life. There are no *"accidents"* in the life of one who has made this commitment. The Scripture says concerning Jesus:

"The Word was made flesh, and dwelt among us...."
John 1:14

The Word of God is never ours until it has been *personalized* in our life experience. Only then can we, with authority, witness to its truth and power. While Jesus was being baptized by John, as He came up out of the water, the heavens opened and the Spirit of God, *as a dove*, descended and settled upon Him. Then the Father spoke:

"This is My beloved Son, in whom I am well pleased...."
Matthew 3:17

This was a tremendous blessing, but there was something more for Jesus to experience before this Word that He received from His Father could become *"flesh"* and *"power."*

Jesus came up out of the water *"full"* of the Holy Spirit. He had received the impartation and blessing. Now, the Word that had been spoken over Him had to become personalized, or made *"flesh"* within His life experience. The next thing the Scripture says is that Jesus was *"compelled"* by the Holy Spirit to go into the wilderness (Mark 1:12). There, He was tested for forty days, *"forty"* being the number of testing. By the end of this time, Jesus had overcome every temptation and had defeated Satan. Now, He was able to come out from the wilderness - in the *"power"* of the Spirit.

"And Jesus being full of the Holy Spirit returned from Jordan, and was led by the Spirit into the wilderness. And Jesus returned in the power of the Spirit into Galilee...." Luke 4:1, 14

The *"fullness"* became *"power"* because truth had become personalized in His life through experience.

"For we are His workmanship, created in Christ Jesus to good works, which God has before ordained that we should walk in them." Ephesians 2:10

We will be able to more readily submit to these *"good works"* when we understand that we are the *"product"* (*we are His workmanship*) that the Lord is producing (*created... to good works*). He works in our lives with the specific goal of making us *"conformable"* to the image and likeness of His Son, the Lord Jesus Christ, that we might become the *"expression"* of His life in the earth, in our day and time.

> **"For whom He did foreknow, He also did predestinate** *to be* **conformed to the image of His Son....."** Romans 8:29

The Lord is bringing forth those who are willing to be tested and proven in order to become all that He has determined them to be. To do this, we must buy of Him *"gold tried in the fire"* (Revelation 3:18). He is searching for those who are no longer spiritually lazy, nor content to rest in the blessings and gifts of the Spirit alone, which they have freely received. Rather, He actively seeks and is knocking on the heart door of those who desire to go further.

These are willing to go into the wilderness and face intense hunger, until they are fed by the Lord Himself. Afterward, they will come forth victorious, in the *power* of the Spirit, to rise into this higher realm of identity with Him in the outworking of His purposes.

Acts 1:8 tells us, *"But you shall receive power after....."* *Power* in our Christian experience does not come as a result of receiving the *fullness* of the Spirit. There is something more that is required for His power to come into our lives. Jesus received the *"fullness"* of the Spirit in the Jordan, but He was led into the wilderness for a time of testing and proving (Luke 4:1-14). Here in the wilderness, *"the Word became flesh,"* or *"power,"* in His life and ministry.

Now, when Jesus ministered, men became attentive and said, *"Never man spoke like this man"* (John 7:46). Why? Because the Word and His flesh had become *"one"* - His life experience in proven (*tested*) submission to His Father. This is the "*oneness*" that the Lord desires to work into our lives.

If we sincerely pray "*Draw me,*" and make this unconditional commitment to the Lord, "*We will run after You,*" the Lord will accept our prayer and begin His work within us. We will be given the "*Baptism in the Holy Spirit,*" along with the "*gifts*" and "*blessings*" that follow. Also, the "*arrangements*" that are necessary to guide us into our time of wilderness testing will be placed in our path.

As we faithfully pass through these, His Word to us and His presence within us will become more than just a testimony or blessing that we share. It will become "*spiritual power*" that has been personalized within every aspect of our being, because we have come into a unity of purpose and oneness with the Lord.

"And they were astonished at His doctrine: for His Word was with power." Luke 4:32

"*We will run after You.*" If I truly mean this, then I must express to the Lord the substance of the following prayer:

> "Lord, in the totality of my being, *my spirit, my soul, and my body; my will, my intellect, and my emotions*; all that I ever was, all that I am, and all that I ever will be, Lord, I, *all of me*, will respond to Your hand upon, and Your activity within my life.

> "Lord, I ask that the Word, which You have imparted and quickened within me, will be incorporated into my life experience, so I will be in harmony and union with You. In submission and obedience, Lord, I will cooperate with You as You accomplish this; and Lord, please do not pay any attention, if I complain."

"For many are called, but few *are* chosen." Matthew 22:14

Another way to say this is: *"Many are called, but few are willing to pay the price in order to be chosen."* There is a price that I must pay to come into the place where His Word has become a reality within my life experience. Then, when I speak, I can bear witness with authority to His Word.

> **"But you shall receive power after that the Holy Spirit is come upon you: and you shall be witnesses unto Me...."** Acts 1:8 KJV

There is a popular saying that the Baptism in the Holy Spirit is *"power for service."* This is true, but this experience has a higher purpose. The Greek word for power is *"dunamis,"* from which the words *"dynamo"* (*ongoing energy*) and *"dynamite"* (*one big bang*) are derived. The *"power"* in Acts 1:8 is far more than a onetime experience. It is an ongoing dynamo (*Holy Spirit power*), which *"causes"* the letter of the Word to become *"spirit and life"* within us. Thus, we receive this enabling power so that we ourselves *"become the witness,"* rather than just receiving power *"to do witnessing."*

When Moses went up into the mount, the children of Israel said, *"All that the Lord has said, we will do, and be obedient"* (Exodus 24:7). This was a tremendous expression of intention, but they failed. The Old Testament is written as a testimony that flesh cannot fulfill the law of God. Therefore, the promise of a New Covenant was given.

> **"A new heart also will I give you, and a new spirit will I put within you: and I will take away the stony heart out of your flesh, and I will give you a heart of flesh. And I will put My Spirit within you, and <u>cause</u> you to walk in My statutes, and you shall keep My judgments, and do** *them***."** Ezekiel 36:26-27

The *Baptism in the Holy Spirit* is given as the fulfillment of this prophetic promise in Ezekiel. It is the power of the Holy Spirit that causes, or enables us to walk, and to continue walking, in His statutes. The word *"power"* in Acts 1:8 has the same meaning as the word that is translated "*cause*" in Ezekiel 36:27. These are one and the same in their intent and effect.

Thus, the Baptism in the Holy Spirit is far more than "*power for service.*" Christian service is something that I "*do*" for the Lord. However, this verse does not say anything about doing; rather, it says that I am to "*be*" a witness. "*Being*" speaks of what I am, rather than what I do.

My being a "*witness*" then, is the expression of what I have "*become*" in Him. If I am "*doing*" witnessing, I am telling someone about the Lord. However, "*being*" a witness means something far deeper. What I am "*seen*" to be becomes very important. In "*being*" this witness, I am saying or doing exactly what Jesus would say or do, if He were here.

The Greek word that is translated "*witness*" is "*martus,*" or martyr. Therefore, I am a "*sample*" (*a living martyr*) of Him; or better, I have died to my life so I can become the "*expression*" of His life in the earth at this present time. This Baptism will truly enable us to serve Him better, but the deeper intent is that through the power that is imparted into our lives, we personally become a *witness* that can be seen as well as heard.

That which I have experienced and become is reflected through my conduct. Now, my life will be a witness of these things. When Philip said, "*Show us the Father,*" Jesus' reply was, "*He that has seen Me, has seen the Father*" (John 14:8-9). Jesus was saying, "*My life is a witness of the Father to such an extent that if you have seen Me, you have seen the Father.*"

When the Lord is satisfied that we truly intend to "*run after Him,*" then His processing will begin in our lives. Jesus said, "*You shall receive power after.*" Notice that the "*Baptism in the Holy Spirit*" is a gift, but the "*power*" is conditional. It is only available to us, "*after.*" We must go through a time of testing in order to obtain the fullness of this power.

In the Song of Solomon, the work of preparing the Bride *begins* at the point where most Christians have become satisfied, and seek to go no further. The Scripture says, *"My people are destroyed for lack of knowledge"* (*Hosea 4:6*). In some meetings, the Lord's people are led to make a consecration, and then are left there until the next speaker comes along and leads them to make yet another consecration. This pattern is repeated again and again, with no direction to lead them further. This is often the reason why many, who are spiritually hungry, feel frustrated as they have a deep inner sense that there is *more.*

We asked the Lord to *"draw us."* Then, we consecrated our lives to *"run after Him."* But, this is not the end. There is yet another step that we are to take.

"...the King has brought me into His chambers...."
Song of Solomon 1:4

As I enter this place of *"intimacy"* in personal communion with Jesus, I will receive (*as a result of my overcoming victory in being tested and proven*) the *"enabling power"* that will strengthen and guide me through the steps that will prepare me to become His Bride. As I ascend into the *"deeper"* realms within His chambers, I will experience increasing degrees of fellowship with Jesus, as being my Heavenly Bridegroom, knowing that I can trust Him to gently lead me through these experiences.

In order to receive the strength (*grace*) and gain the capacity (*willingness*) that I will need during these times of testing, I will be drawn upward into His chambers to spend time alone with Him in the intimacy of His presence. As I bask in His presence and *"wait"* upon Him, I will receive this enabling power (Acts 1:8). The time that I spend waiting upon the Lord is of utmost importance. This is why the power is given, *"after."*

"He gives power to the faint; and to them that have **no might He increases strength. Even the youths shall faint and be weary, and the young men shall utterly fall. But they that wait upon the Lord shall renew** their

29

strength: they shall mount up with wings as eagles; they shall run and not be weary; *and* **they shall walk, and not faint."** Isaiah 40:29-31

"The King has brought me into His chambers." Herein is the secret: I must spend time in communion with my Lord. When I enter His chambers and *"wait"* in His presence, the *power* of God will flow into my spirit. Only then will I be able to *"go into the vineyard"* with the Lord in the outworking of all that I have received. I may become weary, but *"they that wait upon the Lord shall renew their strength."*

It is essential to our spiritual health that we spend quality time in His presence, waiting upon Him. Only then will we have the spiritual energy to face the challenges, testings, and problems of life.

Our Heavenly Bridegroom desires to bring us into *"His chambers"* to abide with Him. Here, as His Bride, we will experience joy unspeakable, unknown to others. During these times of *intimate fellowship*, we are brought into a closer union with Him. In the closeness of this communion, we will receive His life and strength, and along with this, we will come into a deeper understanding of spiritual principles - the unfolding of His Word, which will draw us yet closer. There is no end!

"After this I looked, and, behold, a door *was* **opened in heaven: and the first voice which I heard** *was* **as it were of a trumpet talking with me; which said, Come up here, and I will show you things which must be hereafter."** Revelation 4:1

As I pray this short, yet powerful prayer, *"Draw me,"* I am opening the way that will lead me upward into the inexhaustible chambers of heaven. Here, as the hunger within finds its full satisfaction, all that I had longed for will be found in Him.

"...the King has brought me into His chambers...."
Song of Solomon 1:4

Chapter 3

AN OVERALL VIEW

Our seeing Jesus as being a Heavenly Bridegroom who seeks the attention and affection of His Bride, will give us a better understanding of the principles that will help in our desire to better relate to Him, and also, to grow toward spiritual maturity.

As we prayerfully follow the steps that Jesus takes in order to draw His Bride to Himself, we also will be drawn into a closer personal relationship with Him. We will become more *responsive* when He comes to knock upon the door of our heart, and more *submissive* to His dealings within us, as we identify ourselves with the reluctant and preoccupied Bride who lives within the pages of the Song of Songs.

As we "*meditate*" upon her experiences while she progresses from being *self-centered* and *satisfied*, into becoming all that her Heavenly Bridegroom desires her to be, and we *recognize* her problems as also being ours, we will be able to more readily submit ourselves to Jesus, as He seeks to draw us into a closer, more intimate relationship with Himself. If we will carefully observe the gradual changes that take place within her, and prayerfully follow her as she moves, *step upon step*, upward toward His chambers, we will discover the delight of joining her, in union and communion with Him.

Also, as we consider the necessary role of the Daughters of

Jerusalem in *"helping"* - by *provoking* the Bride to become all that the Bridegroom desires her to be, we will be able to better understand and appreciate our relationship to other Christians. We will recognize that their role is similar to that of the Daughters of Jerusalem, as they expose our need (*their criticisms*) by providing us with opportunities to *"overcome"* in the development of our spirituality.

We can quicken the pace of our spiritual growth by becoming more spiritually *sensitive* than we presently are, which will help us to more quickly hear and respond to the beckoning call of our *"Heavenly Bridegroom."* Also, the level of our spirituality will be affected by how we see ourselves in relation to the *"Daughters of Jerusalem"* (*spiritual pride*). If we are not able to *"overcome"* the obstacles they place in our path, the Lord may wait until we are ready.

> **"I charge you, O you Daughters of Jerusalem, by the roes, and by the hinds of the field, that you stir not up, nor awake *My* love, till she please."** Song of Solomon 2:7
> (she - NAS margin)

The Lord will never deal with us, or allow others to *"affect"* us, beyond that which we can handle. He knows the rate at which we can successfully progress spiritually. It is very important that we recognize this. Also, we must deal with any spiritual pride that may have developed within us, especially if we begin to feel more spiritual than others.

As we compare our hesitations in responding to our Heavenly Bridegroom with those of the Bride, we will realize how far we have strayed from abiding in Him. This will stir us to earnestly pray, as she did, *"Draw me,"* and then make the commitment that she made, *"We will run after You."* This most important prayer, asking the Lord to *enlarge* our spiritual hunger and to *strengthen* our consecration to follow Him alone, will release our Heavenly Bridegroom to change us into the Bride that He longingly desires us to become.

No longer will we view the Lord merely as being the Supreme Power to whom we pray, in an attempt to cause Him to do as we desire. We will begin to relate to Him experientially, as being a *"divine friend"* who personally loves us and greatly desires our fellowship. As we look forward to our times of communion with Him, and as we respond to the expression of His love reaching toward us, we will feel, deep within the totality of our being, a sense of satisfaction and fulfillment.

We were created with the *ability* (*spiritual sensitivity*) to respond to our Lord. In creation, God built within us the *capacity* to enter into intimate, personal communion with Him. Thus, He *"calls"* to awaken this desire within us.

"Deep calls to deep...." Psalm 42:7

There is a *"depth"* in God that seeks satisfaction. The vastness of the universe expresses this desire, as He searched throughout all that He had created, but could not find the fulfillment He sought. Therefore, He returned and created man with a *depth* of potential within him. Here, our Lord seeks to find the satisfaction that He longs for, through times of communion with us.

By divine intention, it is not possible for us to find spiritual satisfaction or fulfillment in anything less than a developing love relationship with Jesus.

Three key *"testimonies"* reveal the progressive levels of spiritual growth to which the Bride has developed. Each of these three confessions of her spiritual condition sets the stage for the intervention of the Lord to draw her further up the *"stairs"* to the next level. The first testimony relates to her feelings of *self-importance*:

"My Beloved *is* **mine, and** (*then, as an afterthought*) **I** *am* **His...."** Song of Solomon 2:16 (comment added)

In her second testimony, some progress is evident, because a partial change in her priorities has taken place. Now she is able to put Him first and say:

> **"I am my Beloved's** (*but adds*) **and my Beloved** *is* **mine...."**
> Song of Solomon 6:3 (comment added)

Although weakened, an element of *self-centeredness* still rules her priorities.

Her third testimony expresses a total change. The Lord has now become her all in all.

> **"I** *am* **my Beloved's and His desire** *is* **toward me."**
> Song of Solomon 7:10

Her *self-life* has been completely dealt with and no longer controls either her desires or her actions.

Notice the complete reversal of positions in the progression of these testimonies which represent her spiritual condition. In her first confession, "*My Beloved is mine,*" she is serving the Lord for her own benefit. She admits that she loves Him because He gives her the things she wants. This reveals a selfish, or self-serving attitude toward the Lord:

> **"Because of the savor of Your good ointments, Your name** *is as* **ointment poured forth, therefore do the virgins love You."** Song of Solomon 1:3

Her request, "*Stay me with flagons, comfort me with apples: for I am sick of love*" (Song of Solomon 2:5), reveals that she views the Lord on a far lower plane of experience than He desires for her. He seeks her fellowship while she seeks that which He can supply to please her.

In her third testimony, she is able to say, "*I am my Beloved's, and His desire is toward me*" (Song of Solomon 7:10). Finally, He has become the center of her life. Instead of possessing the Lord (*religious*), she is possessed by Him (*spiritual*). She has left the place of self-centeredness where she tried to use the Lord for her own purposes. Now, she has submitted her life to Him that she might *live and move* in continual fellowship and communion with Him.

This has opened a way of entrance into His *"chambers,"* where she might become a partaker with Him in the outworking of His plan and purpose for mankind, now and in the ages to come.

Often, in the beginnings of our Christian experience, we become spiritually satisfied because of the many blessings that we receive. We could easily turn aside and rest in these and remain in a lower level of identity with Jesus, as being one of the Daughters of Jerusalem.

Instead, as we respond to our spiritual hunger, no matter how little it may be, and ask the Lord to draw us yet closer, we will be introduced by the Holy Spirit to the Person (*Jesus*) who gave all these *"blessings"* to us. As we fellowship with Jesus, He will gently correct (*chasten*) us in order to lead us beyond our initial experience in which we had become content with just receiving *"things"* from Him.

As we become *one* with Him - within His chambers, we will enter into a much deeper realm of purpose and fulfillment in which we become the expression of His life in the earth. Now, we are ready to have a part with Him in the building up of others, and in the establishing and outworking of His purposes.

During the initial stage of our spiritual life, when our experiences were centered upon receiving from the Lord, we expressed our appreciation, telling Him that we *"loved"* Him. This love, however, related to and was the direct result of the blessings that we were receiving. The *center* of our relationship to the Lord was in *"getting."*

As we grew spiritually, this expression of love took a different direction. Our *"love"* for the Lord began to center upon Him as a person, which resulted in a desire to bring others into the same experience that we had received from Him. Now, the center of our relationship to the Lord has changed to *"giving."*

There are three different Greek words used to express this one English word *"love."* The first, or the lowest Greek word for *"love"* is *eros.* This word expresses a one-way love that moves toward us. It is a love that is self-seeking. It is carnal or sensual, the lowest form of love. This Greek word for *"love"* is not used in the Bible.

The second Greek word for *"love"* is *phileo.* This word expresses the highest type of *"human love."* This is a *"love"* that is reciprocated, or a love that responds to love, and flows two ways.

> **"I love them that love Me; and those that seek Me early shall find Me."** Proverbs 8:17

The third and highest Greek word for *"love"* is *agape.* This is the word that is used to express *"divine love"* and speaks of sacrifice. It also expresses a one-way love, but it is an outgoing, selfless, giving love that looks for nothing in return.

> **"For God so loved the world, that He gave His only begotten Son...."** John 3:16

In the New Testament, there is an illustration of the use of the latter two words for love, *phileo* and *agape.* John 21:15-18 gives the account of Jesus restoring Peter, after Peter had denied Him.

The Lord asked Peter, *"Love you Me?"* And Peter replied, *"Yea Lord, You know that I love You."* Jesus repeated, *"Love you Me?"* and Peter said, *"Yea Lord, You know that I love You."* And then, the third time, Jesus said, *"Love you Me?"* and Peter was grieved and responded, *"Lord, You know all things, You know that I love You."*

The unfolding of Peter's confession that led to his grief is quite different in the expression of the Greek language, than is revealed in English. Peter had previously told the Lord, *"Though I should die with You, yet will I not deny You"* (Matthew 26:35). But, when Jesus was taken captive and stood before the high priest to be judged, Peter denied that he even knew Jesus, because he feared for his own life.

After the resurrection, Jesus came to Peter and said, *"Peter, do you agape Me?"* (*love Me to the point of death*). And Peter responded, *"Lord, I phileo You"* (*I am fond of You*). Before, Peter had said to Jesus, *"Lord, I agape You"* (*I will die for You*). But, when the trial came, Peter failed. He discovered that he was not all that he thought himself to be. Now, he could not use the word *"agape"* because his *experience* was less than his *confession*. Therefore, he had to speak from the level of his experience, so he said, *"Lord, I phileo You."*

Again Jesus said, *"Peter, do you agape Me?"* And Peter said, *"Lord, You know that I phileo You."* Then, Jesus came down to the level of Peter's experience and said, *"Peter, do you phileo Me?"* At this word, Peter broke and cried saying, *"Lord, You know all things; You know that I am only capable of phileo, not agape love."* Because the Lord condescended to Peter's level of experience, his resistance to the Lord melted; and he rose up into a new level of faith and was fully restored.

We all desire the highest. However, each of us must start at the lowest, where the Lord first found us, and then begin to climb, *step upon step*, toward His chambers, gradually developing the capacity to enter within to partake of the highest expression of His love. Thus, the Bride in her first confession revealed her spiritual condition at that time, when she said, *"My Beloved is mine"* (Song of Solomon 2:16). This brought her to the lowest (*eros*) step on the stairs. She is only capable of responding selfishly to a one-way love, which flowed toward her.

The Lord began to bring about changes within her, so she could love Him as a person (*phileo*), rather than loving Him because of all that He provided for her. After He tenderly corrected her, she was able to say in her second confession, *"I am my Beloved's, and my Beloved is mine"* (Song of Solomon 6:3). She has progressed upward on the stairs to the *"phileo"* level of experience. She is responding to His love and beginning to notice Him as a person, but she is still very interested in all of the blessings and gifts that are available to her.

Finally, He drew her further up the stairs, toward the level of spiritual maturity in which she was able to say, *"I am my Beloved's and His desire is toward me"* (Song of Solomon 7:10). Now her love has become an outgoing love (*agape*) with no expectancy of return. The Lord has become her all in all, and she has entered into an abiding *oneness* in Him, in which she shares in His love (*agape*) that reaches out to the world.

In undivided submission, devotion, and rest, she has reached the place in her spiritual growth where she is able to move with Him in ministry to the needs of others, or, abide alone with Him in intimate communion. Therefore, He is able to say to her:

> **"Come, My beloved, let us go forth into the field; let us lodge in the villages. Let us get up early to the vineyards; let us see if the vine flourish,** *whether* **the tender grape appear,** *and* **the pomegranates bud forth; there will I give you My loves."** Song of Solomon 7:11-12

Suddenly, all of the pain and loss she had to endure to become His Bride has faded into nothingness. Now she only sees the vineyard that is before them. Together, they will go forth into this vineyard to minister to others in love, while experiencing new dimensions of communion together.

> **"...there will I give you My loves."** Song of Solomon 7:12

Chapter 4

OUR SPIRITUAL POTENTIAL

The *methods* that the Lord uses to bring us into the level of spiritual maturity that He desires for us are progressively laid out, *step upon step*, within the Song of Solomon. These *spiritual principles* are available to, and will work for, all those who prayerfully seek to understand the *"ways of the Lord,"* with a sincere desire to apply this higher realm of divine relationship to their life experience.

As we experientially identify ourselves with the Bride and partake with her in the many *"reductions"* that she experiences in qualifying to become His Bride, we also will be changed and become *one* in agreement with those who will emerge as His Bride, at the coming *"marriage supper of the Lamb."*

> **"And he says to me, Write, Blessed *are* they which are called to the marriage supper of the Lamb. And he says to me, these are the true sayings of God."** Revelation 19:9

Even though her first testimony, *"He is mine,"* indicates that she was very immature and quite selfish, the Bridegroom saw the *potential* within her, and longed to make her His Bride. It is encouraging to know that any *"seeming"* deficiency in our spirituality will not hinder the Lord from drawing us to Himself.

This can be seen in the initial steps that were taken by the Bridegroom to establish a personal relationship with His potential Bride, despite her *self-serving* responses to Him. This process began as He sought to draw her to Himself by expressing His love for her through His "*Song of Songs.*"

"The song of songs, which *is* Solomon's." Song of Solomon 1:1

The Bride responded to His "*Song of Love*" by expressing her desire for intimate communion with Him:

"Let Him kiss me with the kisses of His mouth: for Your love *is* better than wine." Song of Solomon 1:2

But she spoiled the beauty of this expression by stating the reason for her love:

"Because of the savor of Your good ointments, Your name *is as* ointment poured forth, therefore do the virgins love You." Song of Solomon 1:3

Notice the *self-centered seeking* that is exposed through her response: "*The reason I love You is because of the many things with which You bless me.*" However, the Lord looked beyond her present immaturity to the sincere hunger of her heart, which she had expressed to Him in her prayer, "*Draw me, we will run after You*" (Song of Solomon 1:4). Understanding this, He responded to her *true need*, rather than to her present spiritual condition and desires.

Anticipating the time when she would desire Him, apart from anything that He might do for her, Jesus began to gently guide her toward the entrance to the stairs that would lead her upward into His chambers (*His manifest presence and glory*). He knew that as she matured spiritually, her desires and expressions would change and become more pleasing to Him. Then He Himself would become the center of her life, rather than the many superficial things she presently sought.

Our testimony often reveals our spiritual condition. Also, it may express some of the hindrances to our spiritual maturity, just as the Bride's confession to the Daughters of Jerusalem revealed the reason for her lack of spiritual growth.

"I *am* **black, but comely, O you Daughters of Jeru-salem, as the tents of Kedar, as the curtains of Solomon. Look not upon me, because I** *am* **black, because the sun has looked upon me: my mother's children were angry with me; they made me the keeper of the vineyards;** *but* **my own vineyard have I not kept."** Song of Solomon 1:5-6

This *"vineyard"* is a type of the Body of Christ; He is the vine, we are the branches. These branches must be *properly* joined to the vine, as their continuing life and health is dependent upon the strength they draw from it.

The problem is that the Bride has attached herself to *"another"* branch - my mother's children (*the Daughters of Jerusalem*), rather than joining herself to the *"vine"* (*the Bridegroom*). In effect, she is saying, *"I have centered my life in those who represent the Lord* (*my mother's children*), *and I have labored long and hard for them, even in the heat of the day* (*black, she is sunburned*). *Then, I realized that although I had worked more diligently than others, I was neglecting my own vineyard."*

She has come to realize that working *for* the Lord, even with intense zeal, cannot satisfy the spiritual hunger that the Lord has placed within her. She has been given a revelation of His presence, and is beginning to desire Him, above all that she could do for Him.

Notice that she charged *"my mother's children"* (*those who were very close to her*) as being angry with her. The Lord may use unexpected methods to provoke feelings of restlessness within us, to cause us to move away from our dependencies and begin our solitary ascent up the stairs toward His chambers (*an open door into His presence*).

We must understand and accept the fact that the more we

progress spiritually, the more lonely it will become. Thus, we must avoid judging or criticizing ministries (*the Watchmen* - Song of Solomon 5:7), or other Christians (*the Daughters of Jerusalem*), whom the Lord uses to produce this discomfort.

Recognizing her spiritual barrenness (*a closed door into His presence*), she cried out to the Lord:

> **"Tell me, O You whom my soul loves, where You feed, where You make** *Your flock* **to rest at noon: for why should I be as one that turns aside by the flocks of Your companions?"** Song of Solomon 1:7

She had become so busy and self-reliant that she failed to recognize His voice when He sought to direct her path to Himself. Now, the Lord has arrested her attention and she is ready to listen. He used the "*Daughters*" - those close to her, to chasten her.

She has learned that she needs *more* than just being blessed by the overflow of someone else's spiritual experience (*the flocks of Your companions*). She understands that being fed by the testimony or ministry of another is good, but not sufficient to meet her deepest need. She has come to the place in her spiritual development where she realizes that it is essential for her to personally and intimately know Jesus.

She must abide in Him, or die. With intense desire, she longs to know what she should do, and asks the Lord for guidance:

> **"Tell me...."** Song of Solomon 1:7

He quickly answers her:

> **"If you know not, O you fairest among women, go your way forth by the footsteps of the flock, and feed your kids beside the shepherds' tents."** Song of Solomon 1:8

The Lord instructed her to search out those who are of "*like spirit*" to Him, who truly know and walk with Him (*footsteps of the flock).* She is to find and follow them, as they will lead her to Him (*the shepherd's tent*), rather than to themselves.

The intense spiritual hunger, which is stirring the Bride at this time, has captivated the Lord's attention. Her enlightened and expressed desire to personally know Him has caused Jesus to turn aside from the *"Daughters of Jerusalem"* to seek her alone, as His potential Bride. She has come to the place where she is determined to intently follow after Him. Because of her newly acquired singular desire toward Him, the Lord has reciprocated by singularly turning His interest toward her. Now, He will begin to cultivate a special relationship with her. His *"approbation"* (*divine favor*) now rests upon her.

> **"There are... virgins without number. My dove, My undefiled is** *but* **one...."** Song of Solomon 6:8-9

Therefore, He spoke a very encouraging word to her:

> **"I have compared you, O My love, to a company of horses in Pharaoh's chariots."** Song of Solomon 1:9

This becomes a very powerful and penetrating compliment when it is properly understood. Challenged by the spiritual potential that has been dormant within her, the Lord is revealing His intention to bring forth from within her, the very best.

At that time, Pharaoh was the greatest of the world's rulers. His agents were sent throughout the known world to seek immature ponies that had the potential to be hitched to Pharaoh's magnificent chariot, overlaid with gold. From among these, the horses that would pull his chariot were prepared through intense, progressive training and discipline.

Then at special times, these carefully chosen horses were hitched to the chariot of the King. In a resplendent demonstration of beauty, harmony, and power, they brought forth the King into full view, displaying him in all of his regal glory.

> **"For many are called, but few** *are* **chosen** (*to bring forth the King of all kings in His regal glory*)**."** Matthew 22:14 (comment added)

Thus, the Lord is telling the Bride that He has seen within her the quality and the potential that will enable her to successfully respond to His training and discipline. By submitting herself to the necessary process of qualification, she will be prepared to become *a part* of those who will bring forth the King of kings in all of His beauty, majesty, and sovereign glory, in the coming day of His manifestation in glory and power (*Parousia*).

> **"When He shall come to be glorified in His saints** (*the Bride*)**, and to be admired in all them that believe** (*the Daughters of Jerusalem*)**...."** II Thessalonians 1:10 (comments added)

The Lord elaborated further, concerning this potential that He has seen within her and said:

> **"Your cheeks are comely with rows** *of jewels*, **your neck with chains** *of gold*. **We will make you borders of gold with studs of silver."** Song of Solomon 1:10-11

Gold is a type of the divine nature, the "*image*" of our Lord Jesus Christ. Silver speaks of righteousness, or right living, and jewels speak of enhanced beauty.

Here is set forth the character and the beauty that our Heavenly Bridegroom desires in His Bride (*and in us*), as He intends to make her *conformable* to His "*image*" (*Gold*) and "*likeness*" (*Silver*). Then in confidence, He will be able to present her (*His Bride*) in open view before mankind, as a "*witness*" (*Jewels*) of His nature and character.

The Bride responded with disbelief and reluctance to His expression of insight and encouragement concerning the potential that He saw within her, as she did not feel worthy, or capable of all that the Lord said about her. Therefore, she replied:

"Behold, You *are* **fair, my Beloved, yea, pleasant: also our bed** *is* **green. The beams of our house** *are* **cedar,** *and* **our rafters of fir."** Song of Solomon 1:16-17

The cedar and fir tree were common in this area. Apparently, her house was ordinary and her bedroom plain (*our bed is green*). She is saying, "*Lord, this potential* (*green*) *that You see within me; that of royalty and of becoming righteous; Lord, all this seems beyond me. I am a simple, ordinary person without any special qualities or abilities. I have very little to offer.*" Then she added:

"I am but a rose from the Sharon, just a lily in the valleys." Song of Solomon 2:1 Complete Jewish Bible

"*I am just one of so many, Lord*" (*there were multiplied thousands of these lilies covering the hillsides and the valleys*). "*Why should You single me out* (*His approbation or favor resting upon her*), *Lord, what do You see in me?*"

The power and contrast in His reply to her is both penetrating and beautiful.

"As the lily among thorns, so *is* **My love among the Daughters."** Song of Solomon 2:2

He is saying to her (*and to us*): "*You may be as you say, but I saw the hunger of your heart. I was moved by your determination to obediently respond to Me when you first prayed, 'draw me;' and by your willingness to change your ways when you said, 'tell me.' You were expressing a longing for 'something more' than your present experience, and it turned My heart and desire toward you.*"

Even though she has no *apparent* ability or talents, the Lord saw the spiritual hunger and potential within her, and He began to draw her to Himself, as His Bride. These *seeming* limitations were not a hindrance to the Lord at all. Rather, He saw these as a challenge to bring forth the highest and best from the dormant spiritual capacity that lay hidden within her.

He had said, *"As the lily among thorns, so is My love among the Daughters"* (Song of Solomon 2:2). This is a beautiful and intense comparison. He saw her as being *more desirable* than all others.

To this she responded:

> **"As the apple tree among the trees of the wood, so** *is* **my Beloved among the sons...."** Song of Solomon 2:3

An apple tree is unattractive, but its fruit is a delight to the physical senses. She is telling the Lord that she sees Him as being like this apple tree, because she greatly desires the blessings and gifts (*apples*) that He is able to give her. Therefore she adds:

> **"Stay me with flagons, comfort me with apples: for I** *am* **sick of love."** Song of Solomon 2:5

She possesses an intense spiritual hunger, but has misappropriated its intended purpose. Rather than waiting for spiritual fulfillment, she is seeking a present satisfaction through natural means.

This is a poor comparison, but it was the best that she was capable of expressing at this time in her relationship to Him. Even so, He was pleased with her progress and continued to give her all that she desired, because He recognized that she had said it out of the sincerity of her heart. Afterward, she testified about His continued goodness to her:

> **"...I sat down under His shadow with great delight, and His fruit** *was* **sweet to my taste."** Song of Solomon 2:3

She has come into a feeling of satisfaction and rest, and spoke of the comfort of *"His shadow."* The Lord had met her need and she seemingly was satisfied with the blessings she had received, even though she was only able to relate to His *"shadow"* at this time. She did not yet understand that His *shadow* is far less than the reality of His presence.

Now that she has come into a time of rest, the Lord patiently waits for her to come to the understanding that she was created for much more than these blessings, which He is able to give her in abundance. During this critical time, He continued to declare His love to her, and then in anticipation, awaits her response.

> **"He brought me to the banqueting house, and His banner over me** *was* **love."** Song of Solomon 2:4

The Lord longs for us to vocally respond to His desire for our companionship. Therefore, He restricts all those who could distract her, that she might discover her need to come to Him alone.

> **"I adjure you, O Daughters of Jerusalem, by the roes, or by the hinds of the field, that you stir not up, nor awake** *My* **love, till she please."** Song of Solomon 2:7 (she - NAS margin)

The Lord is saying to all those who are around her (*including pastors, counselors, and friends*): *"Do not try to please or satisfy her. It is My intention that she will become dissatisfied with her present feelings of fulfillment and contentment with all the blessings that I have given her. I long for her to seek after Me, for Myself."*

There is a foundational spiritual principle expressed in the Sermon on the Mount that applies to the Bride's spiritual need at this time.

> **"Blessed are the poor in spirit** (*those who have come to the end of all self-seeking*)**, for theirs is the Kingdom of Heaven** (*the higher realms of His presence*)**."** Matthew 5:3 (comments added)

We may feel that we are waiting for the Lord, when in reality, He is waiting for us. If we are satisfied with our present level of spiritual understanding and growth, He will leave us there. The responsibility for entering the next step is upon us, for He had said concerning her, *"Do not stir up, nor awake My love until she please*" (Song of Solomon 2:7). When we are ready to go further, He will respond.

As the Bride rested within the banqueting house, satisfied with the many blessings she had received, the Lord continued to speak to her concerning His desire to make Himself personally and intimately known to her.

> **"...His banner over me** *was* **love... His left hand** *is* **under my head, and His right hand does embrace me."**
> Song of Solomon 2:4, 6

This caused a stirring and gradual awakening within her, and she began to desire Him above all else. Finally, she recognized and responded to His presence:

> **"The voice of my Beloved! behold, He comes, leaping upon the mountains, skipping upon the hills."**
> Song of Solomon 2:8

Her excited response stirred Him to begin the next step in preparing her to become His Bride. He withdrew Himself and stood in the shadows, outside the *"banquet room"* of her present experience. She is yet incapable of realizing that His *seeming* withdrawal is actually a blessing intended to bring her up another step, upon which the experience of His *"manifest presence"* will be made available to her.

> **"My Beloved is like a roe or a young hart: behold, He stands behind our wall, He looks forth at the windows, showing Himself through the lattice."** Song of Solomon 2:9

Hoping that she will notice Him, Jesus gently begins to reveal His presence through the lattice. He, the Lord of Glory, reluctantly remains without, *alone and lonely*, longing for her fellowship, while she is within; *alone - but comfortable*, satisfied with all the blessings He has provided. He waits for her to realize that she has been redeemed for a higher purpose and invite Him to come within, that they might sup and commune together.

"Because you say, I am rich, and increased with goods, and have need of nothing... Behold, I stand at the door, (*without*), and knock: if any man hear My voice, and open the door, I will come in to him, and will sup with him, and he with Me." Revelation 3:17, 20

Our Heavenly Bridegroom is not willing to allow us to continue resting in the area of His "*shadow*," being content with all that He provides. He longs to bring us into the *experiential* reality of His manifest presence, so He can make Himself known to us.

"He that has My commandments, and keeps them, he it is that loves Me: and he that loves Me shall be loved of My Father, and I will love him, and will manifest Myself to him." John 14:21

The word "*manifest*" means "*to make visible to one or more of our five physical senses.*" Our Lord's "*manifest presence*" begins at the *point* where we pass from the "*letter*" of the Word into the "*Spirit*" of the Word. We are not ready to enter His chambers (*experience His manifest presence*) if we are satisfied with the fact (*shadow*) that He is always present (*omnipresence*) with us. His quickened (*manifest*) presence is to be greatly desired and highly valued, as it speaks of "*sacred ground*" within His chambers.

Therefore, Jesus knocks upon the "*door*" of our spirit because He desires to introduce us to His *manifest presence* in which He can more fully reveal Himself to us. If we desire to be among the "*wise virgins*," we will set all else aside and respond quickly, when we first hear this knock.

"And while they went to buy, the Bridegroom came; and they that were ready went in with Him to the marriage: and the door was shut." Matthew 25:10

Our relating to the "*omnipresence*" of the Lord includes our feeling a sense of "*divine presence*," but there is more. This is only the "*doorway*" that leads into His "*manifest presence*," where we meet Him, as a *"person."* We pass through this doorway when we acknowledge that He is present and invite Him to come within. Here, as we worship and express our love to Him, He in turn will feed us with that which has eternal *substance* and *purpose.*

When we enter into His manifest presence (*His chamber*), He will lead us to quietly *"wait"* upon Him. As His presence becomes personally real to us, He may make known to us something that He desires to accomplish, and reveal our part in its outworking. He may give us a special insight into His Word. Or, He may share a specific burden of prayer or intercession with those who have, in some measure, experienced *"the fellowship of His sufferings"* (Philippians 3:10). The possibilities are manifold, if we will be patient to wait in His presence.

The Lord has been hurt so many times by those who take His presence lightly that He is reluctant to openly reveal Himself. Therefore, He will approach us very cautiously to see if we really are interested in knowing Him as a person.

> **"...Behold, He stands behind our wall, He looks forth at the windows, showing Himself through the lattice."**
> Song of Solomon 2:9

He longingly looks through the window of her (*our*) soul, seeking to attract the attention of the Bride, to see if she truly desires His presence and fellowship. Finally, when she faintly notices His face (*as a shadow*), she realizes that she can no longer remain satisfied with her present experience, simply knowing about Him.

In full anticipation of all that is about to follow, she invites Him to come within. The Lord's response to this *"open door"* is immediate. He comes within her spirit to sup with her, and she with Him, that she might be *"made ready"* (*preparation*) to rise up with Him into His chambers.

> **"And have made us to our God kings and priests: and we shall reign on the earth."** Revelation 5:10

This separated time of preparation (*have made us*) has created within her the capacity for intimacy in communion with Him, and also, the ability to participate with Him in the outworking of His end-time purposes.

> **"Come, My beloved, let us go forth into the field; let us lodge in the villages. Let us get up early to the vineyards; let us see if the vine flourish,** *whether* **the tender grape appear,** *and* **the pomegranates bud forth: there will I give you My loves."** Song of Solomon 7:11-12

He has something far better to offer her (*us*), if she (*we*) will "*rise up*" with Him into the higher realm of a cooperative relationship with Him. To this He added a word of encouragement concerning all that will take place as she responds to this upward call.

> **"My Beloved spoke, and said to me, Rise up, My love, My fair one, and come away. For, lo, the winter is past, the rain is over** *and* **gone; the flowers appear on the earth; the time of the singing** *of birds* **is come, and the voice of the turtle is heard in our land."** Song of Solomon 2:10-12

The Bride has made a major breakthrough. The winter is past and the "*flowers*" are beginning to appear. A "*spiritual winter*" is a time in which the Lord is *seemingly* absent and we feel little or no "*quickening*" presence. The primary purpose of a "*winter season*" is to cause us to seek something further, rather than remaining content with our past spiritual accomplishments. During this time of winter, we may not be aware that the Lord is *patiently* waiting without, but *actively* looking within.

Our growth into spirituality is dependent upon our receiving from the Lord an impartation of Himself (*manifest presence*) into our innermost being as quickening Spirit. As we experience His manifest presence and glory, we will be lifted from having only *judicial* knowledge, into an *experiential* relationship in which the Lord will become personally real to us.

> **"Taste and see that the Lord is good....."** Psalm 34:8

This process (*His coming within*) is depicted here as the flowers appearing, the singing of birds, and the voice of the turtle being heard. The "*flowers appearing*" speaks of "*fruit*" that results from our growth into spiritual maturity. The "*singing of birds*" speaks of the expression of "*worship*" that flows up to the Lord from deep within us. The "*voice of the turtle*" speaks of our becoming "*prophetic*" in order to give anointed expression to a present Word.

These spiritual qualities cannot be developed through an *intellectual* comprehension of His Word or doctrine, but rather, through a *quickened impartation* of His life to us, as the vine imparting its life into the branches. Only then can the spiritual truths, which have become a personal reality within us, be understood and communicated to others. It is essential that we invite the Lord to come within, and that we give Him full control of the totality of our being.

Any amount of "*spiritual indifference*" that may be resident within us, along with any "*self-serving ambitions*" that we have toward the Lord, will be exposed through our identification with the successive experiences of the Bride in becoming *one* with the Bridegroom. As we witness the correction of these problem areas within her, we will gain an understanding that will help us to submit to His dealings in us. Then He will be able to lead us up the stairs, step upon step, into a deeper experience of communion and cooperation with Him.

> **"He made known His ways to Moses, His acts to the children of Israel."** Psalm 103:7

It is one thing to observe what the Lord is doing; it is another to understand and become involved with Him in the outworking of all that He intends. Paul's longing to be a partaker in "*the fellowship of His sufferings*" was evidenced in his cry:

> **"That I may know Him, and the power of His resurrection, and the fellowship of His sufferings, being made conformable to His death."** Philippians 3:10

The Lord longs to bring us into a higher realm of communion with Him (*that I may know Him*), but the price is high. It requires our being identified with Him in death (*the power of His resurrection*) before we will be able to experience any level of *fellowship with Jesus in His sufferings*. There are many levels (*ascent on the stairs*) of experience available to us in relation to intimacy in knowing Him. When we go beyond this, into an *intercessory* identity with Him, He is able to intercede through us. Now we are entering into "*the fellowship of His sufferings.*"

> **"My Beloved spoke, and said to me, Rise up, My love, My fair one, and come away."** Song of Solomon 2:10

As we respond to His call to "*rise up and come away,*" the Lord will lead us into these realms of experiential identification with Him. Here, *within His chambers*, as we are united with Him as His Bride, we will be enabled to express our love to Him as never before, and also have a part with Him in bringing redemption to the nations.

Nothing that we could ever obtain apart from Him can compare with this.

> **"Come, My beloved, let us go forth into the field... there will I give you My loves."** Song of Solomon 7:11-12

Chapter 5

A SINGLE EYE

"Behold, you *are* **fair, My love; behold, you** *are* **fair; you** *have* **doves' eyes."** Song of Solomon 1:15

The Bridegroom has seen within the Bride a quality that attracted His *singular* attention toward her. She has a *"single eye"* that is focused upon Him. Therefore, He sees her in a different relationship to Himself than the many Daughters of Jerusalem. His favor, or *"approbation,"* now rests upon her as He begins the process of drawing her to Himself, as His Bride.

"Let us be glad and rejoice, and give honor to Him: for the marriage of the Lamb is come, and His wife has made herself ready." Revelation 19:7

There are two different *levels* of relationship in our spiritual development. The *first level* finds its outworking *"within us."* Deep within each of us is a *"chamber within our spirit," <u>which we are to make ready</u>,* and into which we, *"as a Bride,"* are to receive our Heavenly Bridegroom, the Lord Jesus. Here, He will begin the process of separating us from all that hinders our having a single eye toward Him in order to become His Bride.

"But you, when you pray, enter into your closet (*chamber*)**, and when you have shut your door** (*separation*)**, pray to your Father which is in secret; and your Father which sees in secret shall reward you openly."** Matthew 6:6 (comments added)

The *second* level of relationship in our spiritual development finds its outworking "*within His Throne.*" Here, "*as a matured son*" (*overcomer*), we are brought into the chamber <u>which He has made ready</u>, the throne of the resurrected and ascended Lord Jesus Christ.

> **"To him that overcomes will I grant to sit with Me in My throne, even as I also overcame, and am set down with My Father in His throne."** Revelation 3:21

Corresponding to these two levels of "*relationship*" are two areas of "*experience*" in our identification with the Lord. The *first* finds its fulfillment within the depths of our being, the "*chamber of our spirit,*" where we, through our *worship, devotion, and submission* to Jesus, experientially relate to Him <u>as being a Bride</u>.

As we respond to the *seeking* presence of our Heavenly Bridegroom (*Jesus*) and open our spirit to Him, He will enlarge the spiritual capacity that is within us. This will result in our having a gradually developed *ability* to enter into and enjoy quality times of intimate fellowship and communion with Jesus.

> **"He that has the Bride is the Bridegroom...."** John 3:29

The *second* area of experience is encountered in the "*chamber of His Throne,*" where we, through our overcoming *obedience* and *cooperation* with Jesus, are raised up into a place of identification with Him, <u>as being a son</u>.

As the times in which we "<u>over-come</u>" begin to outnumber our "<u>short-comings,</u>" we are approaching spiritual maturity.

This *increase* in our spiritual capacity will enable the Lord to impart to us an understanding of Kingdom principles and how the Kingdom functions. This understanding will equip us for participation with Him in His throne, as a son.

"For whom the Lord loves He chastens, and scourges every son whom He receives." Hebrews 12:6

"If we suffer, we shall also reign with *Him*...." II Timothy 2:12

These *"chambers"* represent the *"ground"* upon which we meet and interact with our Lord Jesus Christ. They refer to our redemptive relationship to Him: as a *Bride,* and as a *son.* In order to properly function in these *parallel* relationships, there must be resident within us an abiding sensitivity to His voice and to His presence. This will require of us a settled, determined, upward *"set"* (*anticipation*) in our spirit toward fully knowing and obeying the Lord.

The *key* to our entering into the full outworking of these two parallel areas of experience is for us to fully open our heart to the Lord Jesus in an unqualified commitment, expressing to Him our love, our trust, and our desire to obey Him. In response, He will meet us within *"the chamber of our spirit,"* so that we, <u>as a Bride</u>, may enjoy times of intimate communion with Him. At other times, He will lead us, <u>as a son</u>, into the chamber of His throne, where we will be enabled to participate with Him in the outworking of His purposes concerning mankind.

"And if children, then heirs; heirs of God, and joint-heirs with Christ; if so be that we suffer with *Him*, that we may be also glorified together." Romans 8:17

The Song of Solomon reveals to us the methods by which the Lord prepares us for these *parallel* areas of <u>experiential</u> relationship with Him. These progressive, *"step upon step"* dealings are arranged by the Lord to produce within us the level of spiritual maturity and integrity that will enable us to become both compatible *with*, and productive *in* our being seated with Him in His Throne, as a *Bride* and as a *son.*

We will be qualified to *"rule"* with Him only after we have first, *fully and unconditionally*, submitted ourselves to Him.

"And he that overcomes, and keeps My works to the end, to him will I give power over the nations. And he shall rule them with a rod of iron...." Revelation 2:26, 27

"And <u>have made us</u> to our God kings and priests: and we shall reign on the earth." Revelation 5:10

"Blessed and holy *is* he that has part in the first resurrection: on such the second death has no power, but they shall be priests of God and of Christ, and shall reign with Him a thousand years." Revelation 20:6

Therefore, our initial seeking should be centered in our being prepared (*have made us*) to become His Bride.

"Let us rejoice and be exceeding glad, and let us give the glory unto Him: for the marriage of the Lamb is come, and His wife <u>has made herself ready</u>. And it was given unto her that she should array herself in fine linen, bright and pure: for the fine linen is the righteous acts of the saints. And He saith unto me, Write, Blessed *are* they that are bidden to the marriage supper of the Lamb...." Revelation 19:7-9 ASV

This time of preparation to become His Bride will begin as we so completely fall in love with Jesus that our fervent expressions of love stir Him to become singularly interested in us.

"While the King sits at His table, my spikenard sends forth the smell thereof." Song of Solomon 1:12

This continuing *upward* flow of the *"fragrance"* of our love for Him will result in our Heavenly Bridegroom taking special notice of us, apart from all others. He will respond to this expression of our love for Him, and in return, assure us of His love for us.

"Behold, you *are* fair, My love; behold, you *are* fair; you *have* doves' eyes." Song of Solomon 1:15

The fact that the Lord so intimately responds to the worshipful expression of our love for Him is a mystery we can little comprehend, but marvelously experience. We should consider His seeing us as being a *"lily among thorns"* (Song of Solomon 2:2), a compliment beyond comparison. Now, in confidence, we can cooperate with Him as He calls us apart for the processing which will perfect us to become His Bride.

> **"...Arise, My love,, My fair one, and come away. O My dove**, *that are* **in the clefts of the rock, in the Secret** *places* **of the Stairs....**" Song of Solomon 2:13-14

The Bride has entered into a personal relationship with Jesus. Because of her single eye toward Him, He has begun the process of separating her to Himself by placing her in *"the clefts of the rock, in the Secret of the Stairs."*

"Stairs" provide a means of ascent from one level of relationship and experience to a higher one.

These *stairs,* and the secret entrance to them, are hidden to all except the Lord makes known the way. They provide us with the opportunity (*possibility*) to ascend from one level of relationship and experience to a higher one, where He desires to bring us for times of intimate communion and fellowship with Him.

Also, our ascent up the stairs speaks of the circumstances which the Lord places in our path in order to test and purify us. A right response to these will result in our becoming an *overcomer*, producing within us a level of spiritual maturity and integrity that will enable us to become spiritually productive in our relationship to Jesus.

In order for us to come into these *parallel* realms of *"communion"* with Jesus as His *Bride*, and a *"cooperative relationship"* with Him as a *son*, we must not settle for less than, or come short of the development within us of a *"single eye,"* which has clear focus and discernment. Our having this single eye is essential, so these *"stairs"* will become increasingly visible and accessible to us.

> **"The eyes of your understanding being enlightened;
> that you may know what is the hope of His calling, and
> what the riches of the glory of His inheritance in the
> saints."** Ephesians 1:18

There are those who have been *"enlightened"* with this higher
level of spiritual perception and understanding. May each of us
be among these.

> **"He answered and said to them, Because it is given to
> you to know the mysteries of the kingdom of heaven,
> but to them it is not given."** Matthew 13:11

Notice that the Lord called her His *"dove"* (Song of Solomon 2:14).
A dove has a very unusual quality; it has a *"single eye."* When a
dove *"sets"* its gaze upon another dove, it is not easily distracted.
For this reason, doves are often referred to as *"love birds."*

Our having a single eye for the Lord will release Him to impart
to us the necessary spiritual perception and sensitivity that will
enable us to enter these *"stairs"* and begin our ascent upward
toward His chambers.

David came to a time in his experience when he cried out:

> **"One** *thing* **have I desired of the Lord, that will I seek
> after...."** Psalm 27:4

All of David's drives and ambitions had been reduced to the
expression of this single desire:

> **"One** *thing...* **that I may dwell in the house of the Lord
> all the days of my life, to behold the beauty of the Lord,
> and to inquire in His temple."** Psalm 27:4

David, who knew he was to become king over Israel, was a man
with many desires. Yet, through the acquired vision of a single
eye, he was able to cry out from the depths of his being, *"One
thing have I desired of the Lord."*

The Lord desires to bring us into this same experience of having a single eye for Him. We were created with the ability to *"focus"* our desires. Our inner man (*spirit*), quickened and inhabited by the Holy Spirit through the new birth, has a newly created ability to respond to His presence, and to come to know Him intimately. All we need to do is become willing to lift the poise (*fixation*) of our spirit upward toward Him. One of the greatest miracles of creation is that an infinite and mighty God finds pleasure and satisfaction in His times of fellowship with us, mere finite beings.

It should be perfectly natural and normal for us to move into the *"deeper things of God"* and enjoy His manifest presence and fellowship (*we were created for this purpose*). By the creative intent of God, our completion is in Him; therefore, it is not possible for us to become complete, apart from Him. When He sees that we long for His friendship and that we are determined to develop a single eye toward Him, Jesus will come to us and say, *"O My dove."* This will be as music to our inner being.

When we become singularly interested in our Lord, the enemy will begin to move against us in manifold ways to distract and hinder us. There are two ways in which we can *"overcome"* this opposition. The first is to press through (*rise above*) this opposition. The second is to maintain such a close relationship with Jesus that He can place us within His protection.

"O My dove, *that are* **in the <u>clefts</u> of the rock...."**
Song of Solomon 2:14

Once we have stirred His desire toward us, He will gently place us within these *clefts* in the rock. This is a specially prepared environment, where He comes to progressively change us, according to our desire toward Him.

This *"Rock"* is the Lord Jesus Christ Himself. Through direct intervention (*clefts*), He will become active in our behalf and begin to remove from us, and from our surroundings, all that hinders our relationship to Him. It is His determined purpose to "*make us*" one with Him, as His Bride. He alone is the Rock Foundation upon which we are to be built and established.

When I first began to seek after the Lord with the desire to intimately know Him, I received an inner sense of knowing that the "*Rock*" was there, but buried deep beneath the rubble that had accumulated during my lifetime, apart from Him. Also, there was an active enemy reminding me of this rubble. Then it was revealed to me that this rubble was separating me from the Lord whom I greatly desired to know. This caused an urgency within me to begin removing all these hindering things from my life, that I might stand firmly upon the Rock.

As we begin to view the Lord with a single eye, He will place within us a strong desire for a washing (*cleansing*) of the totality of our being. As we progressively dig down to the stratum of Rock upon which we will be able to firmly stand, the Lord will empower us to forever dispose of the "*rubble*" that has accumulated in our lives. Once gone, it is important that we "*forget*" these things.

> **"Brethren, I count not myself to have apprehended: but** *this* **one thing** *I* **do, <u>forgetting</u> those things which are behind, and reaching forth to those things which are before, I press toward the mark for the prize of the high calling of God in Christ Jesus."** Philippians 3:13-14

Now, the Lord will be able to reveal to us a new basis for our identity with Him. Instead of standing upon the rubble and debris of many frustrating failures, there will be the "*Rock foundation assurance*" that He will continue His work of fully changing us into the Bride that He desires.

> **"The eyes of your understanding being enlightened; that you may know what is the hope of His calling, and what the riches of the glory of His inheritance in the saints, And what** *is* **the exceeding greatness of His power to us-ward who believe, according to the working of His mighty power."** Ephesians 1:18-19

Chapter 6

FINDING THE PLACE OF ENTRANCE

In order to find the place of entrance to the stairs that lead upward into His presence, we must first dig down through all of the accumulated rubble (*past mistakes and failures*) to the Rock. Here, the first step will come into view and we will be able to enter and begin our ascent. As we progress upward on the stairs, Jesus will become increasingly more personal and real to us. Also, we will begin to see and understand things from His perspective. John the Baptist said:

"He must increase, but I *must* decrease." John 3:30

In effect, he is saying, *"the way up is down."*

"For My thoughts *are* not your thoughts, neither *are* your ways My ways, says the Lord. For *as* the heavens are higher than the earth, so are My ways higher than your ways, and My thoughts than your thoughts." Isaiah 55:8-9

In the beginning of the Song of Solomon, the Lord saw a potential, or quality within His intended Bride and said:

"I have compared you, O My love, to a company of horses in Pharaoh's chariots." Song of Solomon 1:9

As she rests in the security of His presence and expresses her desire to commune with Him, Jesus is becoming singularly interested in her and has begun the process of separating her to Himself, from among the Daughters of Jerusalem.

> **"O My dove,** *that are* **in the clefts of the rock, in the Secret** *places* **of the Stairs, let Me see your countenance, let Me hear your voice; for sweet** *is* **your voice, and your countenance** *is* **comely."** Song of Solomon 2:14

May our Lord also hear our voice (*let Me hear your voice*), as we prayerfully substitute our name in place of her name, and make the commitment that she made.

She has not only given Him permission to work within her as He chooses (*draw me*), but she has encouraged Him to do so (*tell me*). Now, the Lord is ready to take her a step further and gently tells her that He has separated her to Himself (*O My dove... in the clefts of the rock*). These "*clefts*" speak of the "*openings*" that give Him access, or the "*right*" to become active in her (*our*) spiritual life experience.

Another quality that the Lord desires to develop within us is stability. Once we have become free from all of the rubble and wreckage that hinders, or separates us from Him, He will carefully "*set*" us within this "*cleft*" in the Rock - the place of "*entrance*" into His abiding presence. As we enter His rest, His presence will resonate within us as He expresses His desire to hear our song of worship (*The song of songs, which is Solomon's.* - Song of Solomon 1:1). Now we will be able, with a pure heart and a single eye, to sing our song of worship and love back to Him.

While resting in the warmth and comfort of His presence within *the cleft of the rock*, the Lord may speak a word of admonition or correction to us. Whenever He sees within us anything that could hinder the solidity of our newfound fellowship with Him, He will help us to recognize the problem. Then, with our cooperation, He will be free to deal with it. Thus, His admonition:

"Take us the foxes, the little foxes, that spoil the vines: for our vines *have* **tender grapes."** Song of Solomon 2:15

A *"fundamental urge of life"* (*the desire to do as we please*) is resident within each of us and manifests itself as a primary soul strength. Within our *soul-life* is the *"law of self-preservation"* which operates at the root of our Adamic nature. Left to ourselves this law controls us, finding its expression in many diverse ways. The Lord must deal with this *self-perpetuating soul-strength* in order to bring us to the place where we can truly say:

> *"Lord, I give up the right to my own life. I am totally Yours; You may do with my life as You please. I understand what this means, and I will respond rightly as You accomplish within me all that You desire."*

The experience of Job demonstrates to us the power of this *"law of self-preservation."* The Lord allowed him to go through a series of testings in order to bring about the necessary correction. Satan came before the Throne and told the Lord that the only reason Job served Him was because of the blessings he received.

"Have not You made a hedge about him, and about his house, and about all that he has on every side? You have blessed the work of his hands, and his substance is increased in the land. But put forth Your hand now, and touch all that he has, and he will curse You to Your face." Job 1:10-11

The Lord allowed Satan to remove these blessings from Job in order to reveal what he would do. Job's reaction was:

"...The Lord gave, and the Lord has taken away; blessed be the Name of the Lord." Job 1:21

Here, Job was still standing firmly on the Rock. The devil again came before the Lord and said, *"The real interest of Job is his own flesh. If You touch his flesh, then he will curse You."*

> **"But put forth Your hand now, and touch his bone and his flesh, and he will curse You to Your face."** Job 2:5

The Lord then permitted Satan to touch Job's body, but he could not take his life.

In the next view of Job, he is sitting on the ash heap, covered with boils. His wife, friends, and comforters have turned against him, but again Job retained his integrity and his trust in the Lord. He came to the place in which we also must come, in order to break this power of *"self-preservation"* and remove its ability to control our actions and decisions. Job cried out and said:

> **"Though He slay me, yet will I trust in Him...."** Job 13:15

After this experience, Job was able to say to the Lord:

> **"I have heard of You by the hearing of the ear: but now my eye sees You."** Job 42:5

Job has been set free from his *self-life* and is standing within the cleft of the Rock. Now, he can clearly see the Lord, who brought him into this place of vision and understanding.

A person's life can be pictured as being a vessel. If a vessel becomes marred in the potter's hands while being worked on, he reduces it to powder. Then he remakes it into something that is either useful, beautiful, or both, as he sees best. The problem is that we, as vessels in the hands of the *Master Potter*, are not always willing to allow Him to reduce our lives to powder so He can remake us as He chooses.

We must implicitly trust the Lord, realizing that His desire and intention is to form and mold us to bring forth the very best from the potential that He sees within us. If we are to enter the *"Secret of the Stairs"* and move upward upon them, we must be willing for this processing to take place. However, some of us have been reluctant to trust the Master Potter with our lives.

One time, the Lord visited us during Chapel in a very unusual way. He prophetically revealed Himself to us, as being a *Master Musician* who greatly desired to hear a symphonic composition. But first, all the instruments had to be tuned. The discordant sound was horrible as they were being brought into tune. Then the Lord indicated that this is how we sound to Him, until we are brought into unity and harmony with Him. Therefore, He tolerates this terrible noise, knowing that once His instruments (*we*) have been tuned, a harmonious symphony will resound in all its beauty and power.

During this service, each of us was being "*tuned*" in order to bring forth this beautiful musical expression that He longed to hear. Then the scene changed, and the Lord began to express the perplexity of His heart. He knew that some of the instruments were so badly out of tune that it would take a lot of tension to bring them up to pitch. Also, He knew that if too much pressure was applied, the string might snap and that instrument would need to be set aside.

Then came a revelation of the broken heart of the Lord, knowing that the instrument might say, "*If I have to submit to all this pressure, I will quit.*" If we are to go on to be identified with Him, we must come to the place where we will allow the Lord to put His finger on our lives and deal with this "*law of self-preservation*" that is within each one of us. We must come, as Job did, to this commitment: "*Though He slay me, yet will I trust Him*" (Job 13:15).

We must enter the cleft in the Rock, into the workshop (Ephesians 2:10) of our Lord Jesus Christ, and allow Him to tune us, no matter what it takes or how much pressure is needed to bring us up to pitch (*our being in harmony with all He intends and desires for us*).

"...let Me hear your voice; for sweet is your voice...."
Song of Solomon 2:14

The Lord greatly desires to bring forth a melody from within His

Bride as He plays upon the strings of her heart. To accomplish this, He has reached into the very foundation of her being and removed all that could hinder their relationship, or provoke her to turn aside to another. As He gently brings the totality of her being into tune, her life is becoming an expression of beautiful music to Him.

She is able to respond to His presence and worship Him through this *harmony* that has come into her spirit. The Lord will now be able to say to her in anticipation and confidence:

> "...**Rise up, My love, My fair one, and come away.**"
> Song of Solomon 2:10

Chapter 7

OUR ASCENT TOWARD HIM

"O My dove... in the secret *places* **of the stairs, let Me see your countenance, let Me hear your voice; for sweet** *is* **your voice, and your countenance** *is* **comely."**
Song of Solomon 2:14

The Lord *looks* to see whether the "*set*" (*direction*) of our spirit is upward toward Him; then He *listens* to hear from within the depth of our being, an unqualified "*yes*" to His desire to lead us further. No matter where we may be, or what we are doing, our spirit can be *directed* toward the Lord. Each morning, before we begin the activities of our day, we should sanctify our spiritual ear to hear His voice, and ask Jesus to guide us through the day.

"...He wakens morning by morning, He wakens my ear to hear as the learned." Isaiah 50:4

The Lord looks (*let Me see your countenance*) upon our heart's desire toward Him, and He listens (*let Me hear your voice*) for the expression of our unqualified *yes*, flowing up from our heart to Him. This will release Him to bring us into the full "*fruition*" of the potential that He sees within us.

"If you be willing and obedient, you shall eat the good of the land." Isaiah 1:19

To be "*willing*" means that my *self-life* no longer controls my desires and actions. I have unconditionally yielded to the Lord the full control of my life and all that pertains to it. Every part of my being now desires, and is responsive to, the very best that the Lord has for me (*from His perspective*).

To be "*obedient*" speaks of my having a "*spirit of obedience*" resident within me that responds through unquestioning obedience to His requests.

> "...**If a man love Me, he will keep My words: and My Father will love him, and We will come to him, and make Our abode with him.**" John 14:23

Therefore, I *daily* set apart time to "*wait upon the Lord*," for His enabling "*grace*" to become both operative and effective within me. For this newly established heart willingness to find its full outworking, it is crucial that I spend quality time, actively "*waiting upon the Lord*." This will result in my having both the desire and the ability to become "*willingly obedient*" to Him.

> "**By whom we have received grace and apostleship, for obedience to the faith among all nations, for His Name.**" Romans 1:5

Grace is the essential ingredient of the New Covenant (*grace... for obedience*).

> "**A new heart also will I give you, and a new Spirit will I put within you: and I will take away the stony heart out of your flesh, and I will give you a heart of flesh. And I will put My Spirit within you, and cause** (*grace*) **you to walk in My statutes, and you shall keep My judgments, and do** *them*.**" Ezekiel 36:26-27 (comment added)

Grace is the "*divine empowering*" that creates both the desire and the ability to obey (*Acts 1:8*). This capability to daily abide in a "*state of obedience*" takes place as I continually *exchange* my inabilities and weaknesses, for His ability and strength. This exchange will take place as I actively "*wait upon the Lord*."

"Blessed *are* **the poor in spirit: for theirs is the kingdom of heaven."** Matthew 5:3

First, I acknowledge my *need,* and my *utter helplessness to attain it,* and then I wait in expectancy for the impartation of His enabling strength (*grace*).

"He gives power to the faint; and to *them that have* **no might He increases strength. Even the youths shall faint and be weary, and the young men shall utterly fall: But they that wait upon the Lord shall renew** (*exchange*) *their* **strength; they shall mount up with wings as eagles; they shall run, and not be weary;** *and* **they shall walk, and not faint."** Isaiah 40:29-31 (comment added)

When these qualities - *"heart-willingness"* (*our part*), and *"grace-for-obedience"* (*His part*), abide within us and work together in harmony, they will produce and release rich spiritual fruit (*spiritual maturity*).

"If you be willing and obedient, you shall eat the good of the land." Isaiah 1:19

This *"good of the land,"* of which the Lord is speaking, is that total *"area"* of my life, which was brought under His authority when I relinquished all *self-control* to Him, and made Jesus the *"Lord"* of my life. Now, I must daily confirm His total control over my life and circumstances, both for my good, and for His higher purposes - even though this inevitably will have a drastic effect upon my personal comfort and desires. As I look back over my life, I can rejoice that because I did this, I am in a much better position and place.

"O My dove, *that are* **in the clefts of the rock, in the Secret** *places* **of the Stairs....."** Song of Solomon 2:14

The secret of understanding how to approach and ascend the *"stairs"* will begin to unfold as I maintain a right attitude and response to these two words: *"willing"* and *"obedient."*

Jesus expressed this same principle concerning heart obedience when He said:

> **"He that has My commandments, and keeps them, he it is that loves Me: and he that loves Me shall be loved of My Father, and I will love him, and will manifest Myself to him."** John 14:21

There is a *"key"* that will unlock the door that leads to the upward path of the stairs. This *key* has to do with establishing within the depth of my being, an *abiding spirit* of <u>willing obedience</u>. This maturing *"heart obedience"* will increase, as my love for the Lord grows, and as I grow in the ability to trust my life unconditionally in His hands. The right use of this *key* (*unquestioning obedience*) will enable me to cooperate with the Lord as He leads me through the many *experiences* and *dealings* that are intended to change me into the Bride that He desires.

As a result of this newfound spirit of obedience, an inner knowing that I have submitted to and entered the process of becoming His Bride will become a reality within me. Many spiritual rewards will ensue as an outworking of my heart obedience to Jesus, and the *"mysteries of the Kingdom"* (Matthew 13:11) will begin to unfold before me.

> **"My Beloved spoke, and said to me, Rise up, My love, My fair one, and come away."** Song of Solomon 2:10

As I respond to this expression of His desire toward me, and begin my upward ascent on the stairs, I must consider that a *"stair"* has first a riser and then a step, or platform. My ascent toward the Lord must progress one step at a time, ever upward toward Him, riser and step upon riser and step. Jesus awaits within His chambers, at the top of these stairs.

The first riser and step can be called *"revelation."* When a Scripture is quickened within me, my understanding is "*opened*" concerning it (*prophetic revelation*). As I embrace this understanding (*the riser*) and act upon it (*the step*), it will become a personal reality within my life experience.

Now I have come up the distance of the first riser (*the revelation*) and have experientially possessed the territory of the first step (*the revelation experienced*). This will bring me to the next riser and step in the process of my spiritual growth. As I continue this progression on the stairs, I will be directed ever upward toward His highest and best, where I will have a part with Him in the unfolding and outworking of His ongoing purposes.

The Song of Solomon became very real and personal to me through an unusual experience during a weekend ministry assignment while I was a student in Bible School. The Lord had been stirring me to seek Him, and I felt an intense spiritual hunger. After the evening meal in the home where we stayed, I retired to my room and made myself comfortable on the bed with some pillows. I opened my Bible to the Song of Solomon, and as I expressed my heart desire to the Lord while reading, something began to happen which is difficult to describe. I was "*caught up*," as it were, into the Song of Solomon. I became unaware of myself, as the message of this book began to unfold within me.

I became uniquely identified with each one of its actors: First, the Bridegroom, then the Bride, and finally, the Daughters of Jerusalem. I experienced their desires, their feelings, and their interactions with each other. As they each "*lived*" within me, I felt as they did. This lasted, perhaps for several hours, as I waited in the Lord's presence.

After this unusual anointing lifted, I realized that I had entered into a spiritual realm, or "*opening*," in which the Song of Solomon became a personal reality to me. My next thought was, "*Now, I have a revelation that I can teach.*" Immediately the Lord spoke to me, "*When I open My Word, do not rush out and teach it. First, eat it, experience it, live it, and then minister the result.*" The Lord was telling me that the Word must become personalized and integrated into my life experience before I could share it with any understanding or authority.

Thus, the *"riser"* that had led me into this unfolding of Scripture was not enough in itself. It was necessary that I be subjected to the experience of *divinely arranged* circumstances that would *"cause"* this opening of the Word that I had received to become a personal reality within me (*integrated into my life experience*).

> **"For we are His workmanship, created in Christ Jesus to good works, which God has before ordained that we should walk in them."** Ephesians 2:10

These *"good works"* are the Lord's part, whereby He arranges upon the step that is above the riser, a set of circumstances that are designed to bring me into a practical understanding of spiritual principles.

After my experience, I began to comprehend the purpose and the depth of the *"divine intention"* that took place when Jesus entered this world as a helpless baby, in order to identify Himself with man and experience all that man experiences.

> **"Though He were a Son, yet learned He obedience by the things which He suffered; and being made perfect, He became the author of eternal salvation to all them that obey Him."** Hebrews 5:8-9

Jesus *"learned obedience."* He was led into the wilderness where He intensely hungered, but refused satisfaction until it was provided for Him by His Heavenly Father. Thus, He overcame all temptation to act on His own (*self-life*) in order to satisfy His need. Jesus had within Himself a determination to be obedient, with an aptitude for learning, through His being tested and proven, which resulted in His being *"willingly obedient."*

The Word declares that Jesus was the Lamb that was *"slain from the foundation of the world"* (*Revelation 13:8*). Redemption through Jesus had been completely accomplished in the will and purpose of God before the world was created (*riser*). Jesus emptied Himself of the prerogatives of Deity, and, through obedience, *became* the author of our redemption (*step*). That which He *was* eternally (*judicially*), He *became* (*experientially*). Through a total submission to the will of His Father, which was wrought out upon the anvil of His life experience, Jesus experientially qualified Himself to become the author of our salvation.

The "*riser*" expresses His *judicial* position, which He submitted to the will of His Father. The "*step*" expresses the will of His Father being made an *experiential* reality within Him, thereby making it His "*possession*" through "*experience*." We are given a picture of how Jesus was able to "*learn*," or experience these things.

> **"Who, being in the form of God, thought it not robbery to be equal with God: But made Himself of no reputation, and took upon Him the form of a servant, and was made in the likeness of men."** Philippians 2:6-7

Jesus was eternally in the form (*morpha*) of God, yet He took upon Himself the form (*morpha*) of man. He *was* God, but He did not come as God acting like a man; rather, He came "*in the likeness of man*," submitting Himself to the disciplines of life. In His condescension, there is no human heart or need that is too low for Him to reach.

Unlike Jesus, Satan sought his own will.

> **"For you have said in your heart, I will ascend into heaven, I will exalt my throne above the stars of God: I will sit also upon the mount of the congregation, in the sides of the north: I will ascend above the heights of the clouds; I will be like the Most High."** Isaiah 14:13-14

Satan said: "*I will ascend... I will exalt my throne*." Jesus did nothing of His own will, but only that which the Father sent Him to do.

> **"...nevertheless not as I will, but as You *will*."** Matthew 26:39

"Then said I, Lo, I come (in the volume of the book it is written of Me,) to do Your will, O God." Hebrews 10:7

While Jesus was in the wilderness, He was tested in each area of His life experience. He refused to act out of His own will or seek His own good; thereby, He overcame. He became the author of our salvation, not just because it was the will of God for Him - which it was, but because He *"qualified"* when He was tested, in order to become our Savior.

Thus, to *"work out your own salvation with fear and trembling"* (*Philippians 2:12*) means that everything Jesus gained in our behalf on the cross, which is *"judicially"* provided for us, must be *"experientially"* worked into our life experience, so we might become all that the Lord desires us to be. The Word must become personalized (*a flesh reality*) within us, so it can be seen and openly demonstrated to the world, through the outworking of our life experience.

Now, my life has become the expression of His life. I had asked the Lord for His best. This led to an increased hunger and desire for the Lord, which resulted in the *"opening"* of the Song of Solomon to me. As a result of this revelatory visitation from the Lord, I was brought to a higher level (*the top of the first riser*) of spiritual revelation and understanding. But, there is more. The *"revelation"* that I received (*riser*) had to become a part of me in order to reflect Jesus through my daily pattern of life (*step*).

As I arrived at the top of the *"riser"* to enter this *"stage"* of life experience, the step *"crossed"* the riser and appeared to me as being *"a cross."* This cross rested on top of the revelation that had brought me upward thus far, and was situated so I could not enter the *"step"* that was above, until first I embraced it. As I died further to my own ways, I was released into the circumstances the Lord had prearranged for me on this step (*higher level of experience*). As these had their full effect upon me, the revelation that I had received became *"personalized"* within me as a present reality, and *"divine substance"* was added to my spiritual experience.

"Then said Jesus to His disciples, If any *man* **will come after Me, let him deny himself, and take up his cross, and follow Me. For whosoever will save his life shall lose it: and whosoever will lose his life for My sake shall find it."** Matthew 16:24-25

The next riser became a test concerning my *willingness* to be obedient to the Lord. He used my previous revelation and experience (*the riser and step below*) as a means to test me. Through patient suffering, as I submitted to this test, more of the energized *self-will* that remained within me was exposed. Again, as I embraced the cross at the top of this riser, a further (*deeper*) experience of dying to self became personalized within me, and I moved up into yet another plateau of resurrection life and experience in Him.

This pattern of spiritual development and growth can be found in varied forms in each of our lives. As we continue to climb the *"stairs"* in our spiritual development and growth, we will be drawn upward on progressive *"risers"* of deepening revelation, which will be personalized within us, upon the next step. Following this, our present spiritual attainment, or position, will be tested through *"diverse arrangements"* placed in our path by the Lord for this purpose. Thus, it is imperative that we recognize and rightly respond to these testings.

As we ascend the stairs, the *"spirit of obedience"* which is birthed and strengthened through our progressive victories, will become an abiding reality and strength within us. These experiences will lead us upward toward an *experiential* identity with our Lord so that our life might become the expression of His life, as we seek to go beyond our present life experience.

"That I may know Him, and the power of His resurrection, and the fellowship of His sufferings, being made conformable to his death." Philippians 3:10

Now, I am at the level of spiritual growth where I am able (*have the developed ability*) to become increasingly identified with Jesus in the outworking of His purposes.

"Come, My beloved... Let us get up early to the vineyards... there will I give you My loves." Song of Solomon 7:11-12

Chapter 8

TAKING UP OUR CROSS

"...If any *man* will come after Me, let him deny himself, and take up his cross and follow Me." Matthew 16:24

Notice that Jesus used the word *"if,"* because the taking up of our cross is conditional. This cross is something we can ignore, take up, or put down. It is within our ability to either choose or reject our cross. Thus, a physical impairment is not a cross because we can neither take it up nor put it down.

The cross that we *"choose"* to bear has nothing to do with the *"fact"* of our salvation or with our going to heaven. We are saved and we will go to heaven because Jesus bore <u>His cross</u>. However, if we are to grow into spiritual maturity and enter some *"measure"* of identification with Jesus in the *"fellowship of His sufferings,"* then it becomes essential that we bear <u>our cross</u>, whatever it may be. This will take a determined and willing, sacrificial action on our part.

The cross that the Lord uses on one individual is not identical to that of another, because we differ greatly in our makeup and needs. That which works to crucify me, would not accomplish the same in another. For example, I was once in a situation in which my income had been provided. However, the Lord showed me that I was to work, regardless. At the same time, another young man who also desired the Lord's best, needed an income but felt the Lord had indicated he should not work. Because we were quite different in our make-up, the Lord used "*employment*" to deal with my self-life; and He used "*unemployment*" to deal with his.

These two opposites were used by Jesus to bring about the same result within each of us. Thus, we dare not say, "*This is the way it worked for me*," and then attempt to place our yoke upon another's neck. The Pharisees did this. They weighed people down and spiritually killed them by putting a legalistic yoke on them which they themselves could not bear.

Your cross may be quite different from the cross I am to carry. Our Lord was a carpenter, so He knows how to make a "*cross*" that will fit each of us. We must not interfere with the plan of God. In the outworking of these crosses, our own ideas often conflict with what the Lord knows to be best.

> **"For we are His workmanship, created in Christ Jesus to good works, which God has before ordained that we should walk in them."** Ephesians 2:10

In order to bring about a further crucifixion within my life to prepare me for the ministry that would come into being in His time and way, the Lord had to dig yet deeper within my life to deal with the "*self-drives*" that were within me. The law of "*self-preservation*," which works within each of us, was very strong within me, as I had owned two successful businesses.

The Lord dealt with me to sell these and go to Bible School. Since I received a cash settlement, as well as a check each week for the next six years, my income was more than adequate. Therefore, I did not need to work while attending school. During this time however, the Lord dealt with me about my weekly check. I was to give it to a young man for a missionary trip to South America. In obedience, I did so, and soon, my family and I were living on squash that we had picked up from the school dump.

A few weeks later, the Lord told me that I was to go to work. About three miles from the school was a furniture factory that made upholstered chair frames. They paid very low wages for extremely hard work, therefore, they had a difficult time keeping employees. In obedience to the Lord, I applied and was hired at one dollar and five cents an hour. Night after night, I was so tired after working, that I could barely drag myself to the car to get home and fall into bed.

The weather was bitter cold at this time. Often, I was sent in a large truck to a secluded railroad siding where, with only the light of a lantern, I was to unload boxcars of hardwood lumber into this truck. Alone, cold, and tired, as I unloaded these boxcars night after night, my spirit sank lower and lower. Then I was asked to work one Saturday morning because a tractor trailer load of lumber had just arrived. At seven-thirty, I started unloading the lumber, outside in the cold, freezing rain. I felt weary and discouraged, and wished I could be at home in bed. About eight o'clock, the owner came out and said, *"No, no, that is not the way to do it. Step to one side and I will show you."* He started to unload the lumber frantically, as fast as he could. Then he said, *"Do it like that,"* and went inside to rest.

As I stood in the freezing rain, on top of this truckload of lumber, I thought of the money I was receiving each week from the sale of the businesses, which was more than I needed. Why was I here, tired and cold, unloading this lumber? I did not need this job! Also, I knew that the young man who was receiving my money each week was home in bed, warm and comfortable. I literally began to react, as this worked on me. The next step would be to act on the thoughts that came to me. *"All this is absolutely stupid. I am going to tell this man off and quit."*

However, I had told the Lord that I wanted all that He had for me - His highest and best. I had made many extravagant promises to the Lord, telling Him all that I would do for Him. As I stood in the freezing rain upon that pile of unloaded lumber, an intense warfare raged within me. Then a verse from Job came to me, *"Though He slay me, yet will I trust*

Him" (Job 13:15), and I began to melt. I repeated this to the Lord and said, "*Lord, I do not care what happens to me, I am going all the way with You.*"

Just then, something of eternal *substance and value* was created deep within my being - I was changed. A deep inner peace, along with an imparted ability to obey the Lord, developed within me, and I was able to finish unloading the truck. My commitment of the totality of my being to the Lord was literally burned into the fiber of my being, through the intensity of this situation.

Later, as I talked with the young man who was receiving the money, he said, "*Saturday morning the strangest thing happened. I was in bed* (*which I knew*), *when the Lord began dealing with me to get up and pray for someone. It was so strong that I could not escape it; so finally, I got out of bed. Then the Lord gave me a vision of someone in a truck and told me to intercede for him.*"

I said, "*I know who that was,*" and I explained it to him. Now, I truly understood that it was the Lord who brought me through this experience in order to reduce me inwardly, so I would not reject or react negatively to difficulties or testings, and would be able to "*stand*" in a place of pressure. Through my obedience in this situation, a "*spirit of obedience*" (*an aptitude to obey the Lord*) was imparted into my being.

Within each of us, there is a spiritual "*potential*" that the Lord desires to perfect. Therefore, He will carefully begin to tighten the "*string*" in order to tune it to the right pitch that it may sound forth as a pure note of "*music*" in all its beauty (*our acceptance of His will in the place of intense pressure*). If this string were to snap as the pressure increased, all would be lost. However, in my case, the Lord had caused intercession to be made for me, so it would not snap. Now, I understood that I might have quit, collected my paycheck, and gone home; but I would have completely missed that which the Lord desired to accomplish within me through that situation.

"O My dove *that are* **in the clefts of the rock...."**
Song of Solomon 2:14

Within the security of His protection (*the clefts of the rock*), an ability to stand and successfully go through the dealings of God has been developed within me. Now I am able to understand, and also, in agreement with Job, say:

"Though He slay me, yet will I trust in Him...." Job 13:15

This is a law of *spiritual growth*. If we are to progress toward spiritual maturity, then the law of *self-preservation* that is embedded within each of us must be dealt with. Otherwise, the fleshly *"I"* will manifest itself again and again, and will adversely affect not only our spirituality, but also, every area of our life experience. The *"I"* that causes us to protect our self-image and well-being will assert itself and wreck the Lord's purposes for us, unless it is dealt with. There is no easy way to accomplish this. Knowing that it will cost us everything, each of us must make this choice.

"If any *man* **will come after Me, let him...."** Matthew 16:24

On yet another occasion, I had planned to visit a man who intimately knew the Lord and had become a spiritual father to me. The arrangements were made, and he said he would have a special meal ready for me when I arrived. As I headed for the car, halfway between the house and the garage, the Lord clearly said, *"You are not to go."* I halted, as I knew it was the Lord. Then, I reacted and reasoned, *"My friend is expecting me, and he will have a special meal prepared for me. Lord, this is to be a very special time of spiritual fellowship and for weeks, I have been waiting with anticipation."*

With desire and expectancy, I had planned to spend several days with him. But the Lord said, *"You are not to go."* First came intense disappointment; then rebellion welled up, and I decided, *"I will go anyway."* I realized, however, that what I was about to do was in direct disobedience. God had spoken, and this was a cross for me to accept and embrace. The intense desire to go had risen up within me and cut *a-cross* the Word of the Lord to me. But I knew I had no choice, except to obey. Finally, I melted and said, *"All right Lord, I will not go. I will call and tell him I am not able to come."*

As soon as I had accepted in my heart the verdict, and spoke it to the Lord, He said, *"Now, you may go, but you are not going alone. I will go with you, for you are now going in the center of My will and purpose."* This trip became a turning point in my spiritual life. I went, knowing the Lord had accomplished something deep within me through my submission to His Word. A better understanding of why it is important to be obedient to His will was also imparted to me. As I traveled, I had an abiding sense of His presence resting upon me, beyond anything I had previously experienced.

This act of obedience carried me to the top of the riser, and built a step (*platform*) upon which the Lord could intervene within my life. Then the Lord began to work upon this *"platform"* to accomplish all that He desired to do within me, at this time. This visit became very special to me, for while there, I wonderfully met the Lord. From this man, who deeply knew the Lord, I received the understanding that there was *"far more"* available to me than I had previously realized. I received from him an *"impartation"* of divine *substance* that created within my inner being a capacity to more intimately know the Lord. I became aware of a deeper realm of spirituality and principles that would enable me to have a much closer walk with the Lord.

Many times, especially when the Lord desires to use us, He will bring us through a test of obedience. This *"test"* may appear to us as having nothing to do with the outworking of the Lord's present purpose for us. A divinely arranged set of circumstances will be placed in our path, causing us to encounter a very difficult cross, with no possible detour around it. As we climb the riser (*overcome*), it will become a platform (*step*) upon which the Lord may do something that may be different than we expected, but necessary. Our obedience will make a way for this to happen. It creates the *"platform"* that will become a *"door"* (*clefts of the rock*), releasing the Lord to move in a higher realm, involving us.

> **"...Behold, I have set before you an open door, and no man can shut it: for you have a little strength, and have kept My word, and have not denied My name."**
> Revelation 3:8

Some may wonder why the Lord is able to use *"so and so"* the way He does. This is because there is an open door of ascent into the presence of the Lord, which <u>they found and entered</u>. This led them upward to the step (*platform*) that was created through their obedience, and upon which the Lord is doing mighty things through them.

This *"door"* is there <u>for us to find and enter</u>.

> **"Then said Jesus to His disciples, If any** *man* **will come after Me, let him deny himself, and take up his cross, and follow Me."** Matthew 16:24

If we desire to ascend, we must pay the price and begin to rise up, step upon step, together with Him.

> **"...Arise, My love, My fair one, and come away."**
> Song of Solomon 2:13

Chapter 9

THE APPROBATION OF GOD

"As the lily among thorns, so *is* **My love among the Daughters."** Song of Solomon 2:2

The Lord uses this contrasting and compelling imagery to emphasize His love for His Bride. This speaks of the "*approbation of God.*" His singular *attention and favor* now rests upon her life. She has touched His heart and He has become singularly interested in her. In the midst of others, she stands out before Him as though she were the only one.

The most important compliment that Jesus could give is for us to receive this expression of His approbation, or divine favor. This would mean that we have become the recipient of His personal interest, concern, and activity. *We have become His friend.*

It is possible for us to attract (*cultivate*) the attention of Jesus in such a way that He becomes both *singularly* interested in us, and *active* in the outworking of our life experience, as if we were the only person in the universe. This is a divine mystery that we cannot begin to understand. However, it is very wonderful and rewarding to experience.

After the Lord had singled out the Bride from among the Daughters of Jerusalem by comparing her to a "*lily among thorns*" (Song of Solomon 2:2), she told Him that He was as an "*apple tree among the trees of the wood*" (Song of Solomon 2:3).

Her interest was only in what He could provide for her. Then she added:

> "...**I sat down under His shadow with great delight, and His fruit** *was* **sweet to my taste.**" Song of Solomon 2:3

To her, His presence is only a "*shadow*," as she has not yet become interested in the reality of His *personal* presence. At this time, the center of her interest is only in the *things* that she desires to receive from Him, rather than in seeking to know Him, as a person. Thinking that all these gifts and blessings, which He is willing and able to supply, will satisfy the hunger within her, she asked Him for even more:

> "**Stay me with flagons, comfort me with apples**...." Song of Solomon 2:5

The Lord responded to this expression of her desire, and gave her so much that she later said to Him:

> "...**I** *am* **sick of love.**" Song of Solomon 2:5

After she had received from Him all that she wanted at that time, she told Him that He could leave and do as He pleased. Her only concern was where He would be, in case she had a need.

> "...**He feeds among the lilies. Until the day break, and the shadows flee away, turn, my Beloved, and be You like a roe or a young hart upon the mountains of Bether.**" Song of Solomon 2:16-17

At this time, her interest in the Lord *centered* in the things that she was able to get from Him. The reason she desired His involvement in her life was so He could provide for all her wants. Therefore she said:

> "**My Beloved** *is* **mine**...." Song of Solomon 2:16

If we listen carefully, our testimony will reveal the present level of our spiritual growth. If our testimony is as hers, it will expose to us the shallowness of our present desires.

"...My mother's children... made me the keeper of the vineyards; *but* **my own vineyard have I not kept."**
Song of Solomon 1:6

As we become aware of our true need and respond in *"heart repentance"* (*my own vineyard have I not kept*), the Lord will open our spiritual understanding and create within us a much deeper desire toward Him, apart from all the blessings and things that He provides.

Although her testimony exposed her selfish attitude, the Lord continued to bless her. Later, when He saw that she was ready to go beyond her initial *self-centered* seeking, He began, in a determined way, to attract her attention toward Himself, as a person. It is important that we notice the method He uses in doing this.

While she was still very occupied within the *"room"* of her self-satisfaction, enjoying all the gifts He had given her, the Lord began to position Himself in ways that would provoke her to notice Him, apart from anything that He could do for her.

"...He stands behind our wall, He looks forth at the windows, showing Himself through the lattice."
Song of Solomon 2:9

This *"wall"* stands between us and the Lord and speaks of the accumulative build-up of those things which hinder, or separate us from His presence. The *"materials"* that make up this hindering wall include, among other things, our seeking His gifts, His blessings, and the *feeling* of His presence (*shadow*), but desiring nothing further. This will cause a dullness concerning our *"perception"* of His presence as being a person with feelings and desires, who longs to make Himself known to us.

"He made known His ways to Moses, His acts to the children of Israel." Psalm 103:7

As we spend *"quality"* time in intimate communion with Jesus (*as a Bride*), and also, during our times of involvement with Him in the outworking of His purposes (*as a son*), we will begin to understand the *principles* (*His ways*) that govern the *methods* by which He moves in relation to those who are redeemed, and also in His dealings with all His creation.

> **"The secret of the Lord *is* with them that fear** (*reverence*) **Him; and He will show them His covenant."** Psalm 25:14 (comment added)

This *"wall"* also blinds us to the *"inner satisfaction and fulfillment"* (*evident divine favor*) that we will experience as we progress into a fully committed overcoming life, in union with Jesus (*our Heavenly Bridegroom*). We will have no perception of all that we are missing.

The Lord greatly desires to bring us into a relationship of personal intimacy with Him. Therefore, it is very important that we cultivate a spiritual sensitivity that will enable us to both notice (*spiritual perception*) and rightly respond (*heart obedience*) to the *"presence"* of our Heavenly Bridegroom when He comes, seeking to take us further.

> **"Where** *there is* **no vision, the people perish...."** Proverbs 29:18

"He stands behind our wall, He looks forth at the windows" (Song of Solomon 2:9). These *"windows"* represent the Bride's spiritual capacity and vision, and are the *"openings"* through which the desire and the voice of the Bridegroom can reach her. She becomes aware of these *"openings"* that lead into His chambers through being quickened or *"touched"* by His presence when she, from time to time, momentarily recognizes that there is *"something more"* (*Jesus Himself*) beyond all that she presently possesses.

> **"The eyes of your understanding being enlightened; that you may know what is the hope of His calling, and**

what the riches of the glory of His inheritance in the saints." Ephesians 1:18

She is still indifferent to His desire to be with her, because she is not yet aware of the lasting, inner satisfaction of intimate communion with Jesus that is available to her if she will respond and invite Him to come within the chamber of her spirit (*I will come in to him, and will sup with him* – Revelation 3:20).

Therefore, Jesus remains without, seeking her attention through this window (*door*) that would open to her and prepare her for the journey with Him into His chambers (*manifest presence*), if she would look toward Him and respond.

> "*When You said,* **Seek you My face; my heart said to You, Your face, Lord, will I seek.**" Psalm 27:8

The Lord desires our presence, but requires an action on our part to indicate our desire to be with Him. Thus, He "*looks forth at the windows, showing Himself through the lattice*" (*Song of Solomon 2:9*). This speaks of the fact that His presence is always in some measure veiled (*showing Himself in veiled form*), until we respond.

> "**O taste and see that the Lord** *is* **good....**" Psalm 34:8

God is "*Spirit*" and can only be known through spiritual perception and revelation. Thus, we cannot abide the full glory of His presence until we first come into the purity of life that is required for us to draw near to a holy and righteous God.

> "**For what man knows the things of a man, save the spirit of man which is in him? even so the things of God knows no man, but the Spirit of God. Now we have received, not the spirit of the world, but the Spirit which is of God; that we might know the things that are freely given to us of God.**" I Corinthians 2:11-12

The Heavenly Bridegroom, the Lord of all creation, stood alone, outside of all that He desired, patiently waiting for His Bride to notice Him. He longed for her fellowship as He looked through the window, gazing upon her in such a way that she could see His eyes.

Finally, His patience met its reward. She noticed Him and felt the intensity of His desire to be with her. All else faded as she responded and invited Him to come into the *"room"* of her spirit, which longed for satisfaction.

> **"After this I looked, and, behold, a door** *was* **opened in heaven: and the first voice which I heard** *was* **as it were of a trumpet talking with me; which said, Come up here....."** Revelation 4:1

Notice that this *"door"* opened <u>when</u> John *looked.*

Immediately, Jesus came within *"her chamber"* (*a set apart place*) and began to lead her toward the stairs, as He prepared her (*enlarged her spiritual sensitivity*) for intimacy with Him, within *"His chambers."* Here, alone with Him in His manifest presence, she began to experience an ongoing relationship of abiding communion with Him.

Now, her eye is single and her desire is toward Him alone.

> **"...Rise up, My love, My fair one, and come away."**
> Song of Solomon 2:10

His intention is to take her beyond the relationship she had previously maintained with Him, which was built upon her abiding in His *"shadow,"* content with all He gave her and the *"feeling"* of His presence. As in the past, He desires to please and satisfy her, but now He has something far better for her. Therefore, He waited until she noticed and invited Him to come within.

If she is to progress toward spiritual maturity, it is necessary that she recognize her need for Him alone. Only then will she be able to see her true spiritual condition and rightly respond to Him, and to all that He intends for her (*us*) in becoming His Bride.

"Brethren, I count not myself to have apprehended: but *this* one thing *I do*, forgetting those things which are behind, and reaching forth to those things which are before, I press toward the mark for the prize of the high calling of God in Christ Jesus." Philippians 3:13-14

This *"prize"* is our having a personal relationship with Jesus, with His approbation resting upon us.

Chapter 10

UNDERSTANDING HIS WAYS

"For, lo, the winter is past, the rain is over *and* gone; the flowers appear on the earth; the time of the singing *of birds* is come, and the voice of the turtle is heard in our land." Song of Solomon 2:11-12

The *"winter"* represents the time of spiritual barrenness that the Bride experienced while content with the blessings and satisfaction she had received by knowing about the Bridegroom, apart from having a personal relationship with Him (*Jesus*). The *"rain"* had showered these upon her; but they were about to be removed (*over and gone*), as she entered the *"night season"* of her experience.

"By night on my bed I sought Him whom my soul loves: I sought Him, but I found Him not." Song of Solomon 3:1

She again attempted to recreate the past blessings she had received from the Lord, but was unable to find satisfaction in them. Suddenly, she realized there must be something beyond all these things, and began to long for the Lord Himself.

"*It was* but a little that I passed from them, but I found Him whom my soul loves: I held Him, and would not let Him go, until I had brought Him into my mother's house, and into the chamber of her that conceived me." Song of Solomon 3:4

It is here that she realizes that much more is available to her, which had been hidden from her.

> **"And I will give you the treasures of darkness, and hidden riches of secret places....."** Isaiah 45:3

The resultant *"flowers"* speak of the *"fruit of the spirit"* - the spiritual *"substance"* that develops as a result of her (*our*) coming through this night season and entering into the intimacy of fellowship with the One she loves. This *"substance"* is His divine nature imparted within us.

> **"That I (***Jesus***) may cause those that love Me to inherit substance; and I will fill their treasures."** Proverbs 8:21 (comment added)

The *"time of the singing is come."* This speaks of the Bride receiving an abiding prophetic anointing to enable her to *better* express her worship and love to the Lord as she comes into this new realm of relationship and experience (*the voice of the turtle being heard*).

The Lord has all the hosts of heaven to enjoy, yet He longs for us to vocally express to Him our love for Him, and how much we desire to have His presence abide with us. First, He acknowledges her single eye toward Him.

> **"O My dove,** *that are* **in the clefts of the rock, in the Secret** *places* **of the Stairs, let Me see your countenance, let Me hear your voice; for sweet** *is* **your voice, and your countenance** *is* **comely."** Song of Solomon 2:14

He has expressed His love for her (*O My dove*). Now He longs to hear the expression of her love toward Him (*the time of singing is come*), and He tells her how much it will mean to Him (*let Me hear your voice*). After she hears the expression of His love for her, she responds in thanksgiving and in worship. He then tells her that her voice has ministered to Him (*for sweet is your voice*).

The Lord then places her in the security of the *"clefts of the rock,"* so her newfound, singular eye toward Him can be strengthened by expanding her personal knowledge of Him through a further revelation of His person, and of His manifested presence and glory.

She has come to the *"place"* where Jesus can begin to reveal to her the *"stairs"* that lead upward into His intimate presence and the way of ascent upon them. Soon He will hear an even sweeter expression of thanksgiving and worship from her voice, as she realizes that this is much better than her past limited experience of abiding in His shadow. As she begins to express this intense desire and love for Him, the Lord repeats to her the second time:

> **"...Arise My love, My fair one, and come away."**
> Song of Solomon 2:13

As He reveals to her the *"secret of the stairs"* and the way to enter, a problem arises that she (*and we*) must face. She has been satisfied with being spiritually fed by others. And also, she has been more interested in His blessings (*stay me with flagons, comfort me with apples* - Song of Solomon 2:5), than in being with Him for special times of communion and fellowship.

Because she is still not ready to respond to His urgent call to *"rise up"* with Him into His chambers, even though He has repeated it twice, He has no choice except to chasten her, by further limiting her freedom to do as she pleases. There is only one way to accomplish this: it must be done at *"night."*

This *"night"* is a time of (*seeming*) spiritual darkness, when the Lord withdraws the *"feeling"* of His presence and no longer responds to her (*our*) requests for all the things she desires; nor is she able to receive these through the ministry of another. After He did this, we find her very upset.

> **"By night on my bed I sought Him whom my soul loves: I sought Him, but I found Him not."** Song of Solomon 3:1

The blessings are gone, and she is unable to find her way in the (*spiritual*) darkness that has settled upon her. Also, the past "*methods*" that she used to receive a blessing, along with the *ways* in which the Lord used her in ministry, no longer worked. She can no longer feel or sense the presence of the Lord, but she has become aware that she has never been so spiritually stirred or desirous for the Lord to reveal Himself to her, as she is presently feeling.

Her reaction to the withdrawal of His presence and blessing is panic.

> **"I will rise now, and go about the city in the streets, and in the broad ways I will seek Him whom my soul loves: I sought Him, but found Him not. The watchmen that go about the city found me:** *to whom I said,* **Saw you Him whom my soul loves?"** Song of Solomon 3:2-3

These "*watchmen*" are a type of the ministry. Before, she was content with all that she received through them. Now, she is intensely hungry for the Lord Himself and began to look for Him through the experience of others. She says, "*I will rise now and go about the city.*" She seeks Him in all the places where she had previously been blessed, or where she heard that He was present. She searches in vain, for she is unable to find Him.

She found a "*minister*" through whom she had received much in the past and asked, "*Saw you Him whom my soul loves?*" However, the Lord did not permit this minister to help her, for the Lord was seeking to draw her to Himself. He desired to personally "*sup with her,*" alone in His chambers, where He would renew her according to the potential that He had seen within her. Therefore, the only thing this minister was able to say to her was, "*You should pray more.*"

In obedience, she did as she had been told; but nothing happened because the Lord did not permit it (*the rain is over and gone*). Therefore, she felt all the more as if the Lord had forsaken her.

No matter to whom she spoke or what advice they gave, none of these things worked or helped her in any way. The Lord had, so far as feelings were concerned, withdrawn Himself from her.

In her distress, she sought all the more for Him. The intensity of this seeking, without seemingly receiving any result or satisfaction, caused her to cry out with an even greater fervency for the Lord Himself. Now, the very thing for which the Lord had been patiently waiting was beginning to form deep within her.

She was recognizing her need for the Lord as a person, apart from things. She is desiring Him above all else; the *"single eye,"* which Jesus had seen buried deep within her, is beginning to surface and focus. She prayed and said to the Lord:

> **"Tell me, O You whom my soul loves, where You feed, where You make** *Your flock* **to rest at noon: for why should I be as one that turns aside by the flocks of Your companions?"** Song of Solomon 1:7

In the past, the Bride had been satisfied with being nurtured by others. She was content with the blessings that were readily available to her through an under-shepherd, and she had no desire to go further, until the Lord removed these blessings from her.

Now, she intensely desires Jesus to personally come to her, that she might *"sup with Him"* (Revelation 3:20). She is beginning to realize that only the Lord Himself is able to meet her need, and has asked where she can find Him. The Lord heard this prayer and began, step upon step, to draw her upward to Himself.

As you read this, if you will compare your present spiritual condition and desires to those of the Bride, and discover that you also may have settled for less, then the necessity of the Bride going through this experience of *"night"* (*the withdrawal of His presence and blessings*) may also apply to you.

If you are already going through an experience similar to this, be careful to not become critical of the ministries through whom you are seeking help, but are receiving little, or none. The Lord may not allow them to satisfy your longings, because He has a higher purpose for you.

There is a time in our spiritual growth when we should begin to hear from the Lord Himself, and receive directly from Him. We are to be "*under tutors and governors <u>until</u> the time appointed of the Father*" (Galatians 4:2). This "*appointed time*" had come for the Bride. Therefore, even though she sought out one watchman (*minister or spiritual friend*) after another, she did not receive that for which she was seeking. Finally, in desperation, she turned to the Lord Himself, who had been patiently waiting, *veiled* behind the "*lattice.*"

> "*It was* **but a little that I passed from them, but I found Him**...." Song of Solomon 3:4

There had been a time when it was right for her to receive all that she spiritually needed through others. But now (*concerning her*), the Lord caused their "*wells*" to seemingly dry up, for they had no word that could satisfy her. The Lord did this because He was seeking to draw her to Himself. An indication of our progressing toward spiritual maturity is when we begin to hear directly from the Lord, rather than being satisfied with receiving through others.

Now she can say, "*I found Him.*" He had been there all along, but she is seeing Jesus in a different way. He is no longer the "*shadow*" to whom she related in the past. She clearly sees Him and welcomes Him into the "*chamber of her spirit.*" During their renewed time of communion together, the Lord teaches her the understanding of His "*ways*" - spiritual principles and perceptions that will help in her ascent upward on the stairs, into all that He has for her. Then He waits as she begins her ascent upward toward "*His chambers,*" step upon step.

After she stopped striving, seeking out the places in which she had previously been blessed, or heard that He was moving in some special way, and became willing to submit to the process of being separated from past methods of spiritual attainment, her new-*found* times of communion with the Lord gradually became a personal reality that resulted in a deep inner sense of satisfaction and fulfillment.

As her new position of being in direct relationship to the Lord was being tested so it would be pure and firmly established, the Lord again said to her, "*Rise up and come away*," knowing that now, she understood. She is ready to experience His "*approbation*" or singular attention, and to be further changed through her times of intimate communion with Him. The "*shadow*" with which she had once been satisfied has become the Lord Himself.

Some are able to progress beyond that of the spiritual leadership in the fellowship they attend. They can maintain a proper attitude and relationship, as long as their intent is to give, rather than to receive. We should not attempt going on alone in our spiritual walk. We would be as sheep that are led out amongst the wolves. The Lord has placed ministry in the Body of Christ for our good, which is to guide us toward the Lord Himself.

Thus, the proper outworking of this stage in our spiritual growth will result in the Lord Himself being the center and circumference of our spiritual experience, having become our all in all. This should not take us away from our relationship to, or our need for, others in the Body of Christ.

> **"And He gave some, apostles; and some, prophets; and some, evangelists; and some, pastors and teachers....**
> **Till we all come... to a perfect (***mature***) man."**
> Ephesians 4:11-13 (comment added)

As we respond in the right balance to these ministries, a spiritual maturity and stability will develop, and we will be able to ascend up the stairs to the level on which we are able to recognize His beckoning presence (*spiritual perception*). Only then will we be able to respond to His desire for us to rise up and come away with Him.

> "*It was* **but a little that I passed from them, but I found Him whom my soul loves**...." Song of Solomon 3:4

Now she has found the "*source*" of the satisfaction for which she has longed - the Lord Himself. She is ready, together with Him, to go further. Each time that she enters a higher spiritual plateau, there is a further disclosure of "*His person and ways*" to her. These cycles of revelation and spiritual understanding will gradually open to us, one upon another, as we respond to these unfolding *secrets of the stairs* and ascend with Him, until we are seated with Him upon His Throne.

As we respond to this call to "*Rise up and come away*" in union with our Lord, others (*the Daughters of Jerusalem*) may criticize, or act with jealousy toward us (*they also would like to enter this higher realm, but are not willing to pay the price to receive*). Regardless of what their criticisms may be, we must maintain a right attitude and continue to press upward.

> "**To him that overcomes will I grant to sit with Me in My Throne, even as I also overcame, and am set down with My Father in His Throne.**" Revelation 3:21

The Lord has led her through this period of darkness in which it was very crucial that she not become discouraged and turn aside. She has been faithful, and as an *overcomer,* she has searched until she found Him.

> "...**I held Him and would not let Him go until I had brought Him into my mother's house, and into the chamber of her that conceived me.**" Song of Solomon 3:4

She has caught a glimpse of Jesus as being her Heavenly Bridegroom and can no longer be content with less. There, she became wonderfully satisfied in the intimacy of His presence.

Chapter 11

SEPARATED UNTO THE LORD

"Who is this that comes up from the wilderness, leaning upon her beloved....?" Song of Solomon 8:5

The Lord is ready to begin the process of separation that will bring His Bride into the place where He will become *first* in all that she desires. Only then will she be able to trust Him with her care and protection. To accomplish this, He brought her into the *wilderness* for a time.

"Until the day break (*spiritual breakthrough*), **and the shadows flee away, I will get Me to the mountain of myrrh, and to the hill of frankincense."**
Song of Solomon 4:6 (comment added)

There is before us *a new day* in which all that appears as shadows will become clear in the reality of our Lord's presence and glory - to the Bride, and also to us. The wilderness is a place of barrenness and desolation in which the Bride is about to be separated from all that has meant so much to her. During this time of separation, these things will lose their value and become as nothing, in comparison to her newfound desire to be in the reality of His presence.

The Bride has come to the end of her own abilities and confessed her need of Him. In the barrenness of this wilderness experience, the Lord brought before her a very special revelation of Himself.

> **"Who *is* this that comes out of the wilderness like pillars of smoke, perfumed with myrrh and frankincense, with all powders of the merchant? Behold His bed... threescore valiant men *are* about it...."** Song of Solomon 3:6-7

The Bride marveled at this display of His power and might, as she witnessed the desire and ability of the Lord to bring her through the wilderness into the fullness of all that He intends for her. Now she sees only Jesus; all other things have lost their value as she falls in love with Him.

Carefully notice that He had been in the wilderness with her the entire time. Her *"leaning"* on Him tells us that she is coming out of the wilderness changed, fully trusting and totally dependent upon Him. Because she has come to the *level* of fully trusting the Lord, He can begin to deal with His Bride in a further step of separation.

In our spiritual growth and development, there is a progressive unfolding of our identification with the Lord as being a *"particular"* member who has been *"set"* within His Body.

> **"Now you are the body of Christ, and members in particular."** I Corinthians 12:27

Being His *"potential"* Bride, we must be firmly established upon the Rock, the Lord Jesus Christ, who is the foundation upon which we are to be built.

> **"And are built upon the foundation of the apostles and prophets, Jesus Christ Himself being the chief corner *stone*; In whom all the building fitly framed together grows to a holy temple in the Lord: In whom you also are built together for a habitation of God through the Spirit."** Ephesians 2:20-22

Judicially (*legally*), the Lord sees us as being perfect. As we receive the cleansing power of His blood, He can truly say of us, *"There is no spot in you."* We must believe and accept this before He will be able to take us any further. Therefore, He tells His Bride:

> **"You** *are* **all fair, My love***; there is* **no** *spot* **in you."**
> Song of Solomon 4:7

We also have this assurance, as forgiveness, cleansing, and purification are gifts. We cannot earn them, but we are to simply believe that Jesus died on the cross in our place. Then as we walk with Him, that which He sees us to be "*judicially*" will become an "*experiential*" reality within us. This is the miracle of redemption. We believe, and then we become.

After He told her that she was "*all fair*" in His sight, He said:

> **"Come with Me from Lebanon,** *My* **spouse, with Me from Lebanon: look from the top of Amana, from the top of Shenir and Hermon, from the lions' dens, from the mountains of the leopards."** Song of Solomon 4:8

He is making an appeal for her to leave all those "*places*" in her past life that hindered her spiritual growth, and which pose a present danger to her sensitivity to, and desire for, His presence.

Our cooperation with this process of sanctification will determine how far we will progress upward on the stairs (*30, 60, 100 fold*) in order to develop a relationship of intimate communion with Jesus. In love, He will call us away from the *borders* of worldly things with all their enticements.

Our intent should be to get as far as possible away from these borders - not to see how close we can stay to them (*Come with Me from*). He will speak this to each one of us, if our desire is to truly "*run after Him.*"

> **"I will rise now, and go about the city in the streets, and in the broad ways I will seek Him whom my soul loves: I sought Him, but I found Him not."** Song of Solomon 3:2

The Lord permitted the Bride to utterly fail in all her efforts, as she sought Him by attempting to recreate past experiences through which she had been blessed.

> **"It was but a little that I passed from them, but I found Him whom my soul loves: I held Him, and would not let Him go, until I had brought Him into my mother's house, and into the chamber of her that conceived me."** Song of Solomon 3:4

Pictured here in the most intimate detail, is the depth of personal closeness that can be experienced during times of communion with our Heavenly Bridegroom. It is difficult to express this in words, but most wonderful to experience.

Before this, she had been *satisfied* with the teachings, touches of His presence, and the impartations that she received through others. But the Lord had something far better for her. Therefore, He allowed her to become *"dissatisfied"* with all that she had previously known and experienced.

Now she is seeking Jesus, alone. The spiritual *"hunger"* that developed within her through this time of searching has become so intense that she can find no satisfaction apart from spending time in personal communion with Him. Here, she finds the satisfaction that she longed for, as she begins to experience intimately *"knowing"* Him.

Notice that first, the *"old"* had to be removed (*It was but a little that I passed from them*) so she would seek the *"new,"* which is far better. But she had not realized this and sought in desperation to recreate the old.

> **"...He takes away the first, that He may establish the second."** Hebrews 10:9

Our functioning in the ministries and gifts that are available to us is a part of the process of our growth into the *"measure of the stature of the fullness of Christ"* (Ephesians 4:13). All these are a necessary part of the development of our spirituality, but we are not to remain there, satisfied with only working *"for"* the Lord.

As we walk *"with"* Jesus, a growing sense of our identity with Him will develop and our life will increasingly become the expression of His life and ministry. We will learn to give, rather than always seeking to receive. Others will begin to see Jesus, rather than being impressed with us.

As we become more *"perceptive"* in recognizing Jesus as our Heavenly Bridegroom, and as we respond to His desire for set-apart time with us, we will receive from Him substantial impartations of spiritual *"substance."* This *substance* is His very life being imparted into every aspect of our being. We cannot give (*impart*) what we do not have.

> **"I love them that love Me; and those that seek Me early shall find Me... That I may cause those that love Me to inherit substance; and I will fill their treasures."**
> Proverbs 8:17, 21

These *"treasures"* are the very *substance* of His *being*, imparted into our lives and ministry, to be seen and handled by others. Also, through our personal involvement with Jesus in a cooperative relationship with Him in the outworking of His purposes, we will more rapidly grow toward spiritual *maturity* (*I am a wall, and my breasts like towers*). Now, we have within us something to give.

> **"We have a little sister, and she has no breasts** (*spiritually immature*)**: what shall we do for our sister in the day when she shall be spoken for? I am a wall, and my breasts like towers** (*spiritually mature*)**...."** Song of Solomon 8:8, 10

As we respond to Jesus in heart obedience, we will learn how to function in a cooperative relationship with Him (*what shall we do for our sister?*) in which we will have a part with Him in the outworking of His purposes.

There is a progression in which our working *"for"* the Lord will gradually fade into our working *"with"* Him (*Let us get up early to the vineyards; let us see if the vine flourish, whether the tender grape appear* - Song of Solomon 7:12). This is established through *"directives"* (*imparted spiritual perception and understanding*) that we receive during our times of communion with Him, in which we receive spiritual *guidance* that will lead us into a higher level of identity with Jesus Himself, in which our satisfaction comes from Him alone.

> **"Tell me, O You whom my soul loves, where You feed, where You make *Your flock* to rest at noon: for why should I be as one that turns aside by the flocks of Your companions?"** Song of Solomon 1:7

If we begin to wander, or settle for less, we will be *chastened*; but we must first give the Lord permission to *chasten us*. This is a part of our coming to understand the *"ways"* of the Lord. For us to have a right response to each of these requires that we become sensitive and responsive (*tell me*) to His beckoning presence.

If we are sincere in our desire to come into the fullness of an *experiential* identification with Jesus in the outworking of His purposes, the time will come when He will begin to separate us from others, to Himself. During this time, we may be shut away from many Christian activities (*especially television*), so that our spiritual sensitivity and capacity may be further developed as we daily experience quality time alone with Jesus.

It is important that we become willing to set time aside for this purpose and are willing to pay the price of any misunderstanding that may result from our responding in obedience. It is during these times of personal visitation in which we meet the Lord intimately, that we are changed by Him.

One of the most difficult areas in our spiritual progress is our ability to trust the *"faithfulness"* of the Lord, especially if we do not understand what He is doing within us, or in our circumstances. The inability to fully trust the Lord makes it difficult for us to completely commit ourselves into His hands and then abide there, in *rest* and *submission*.

Our lack of trust must be dealt with if we are to go further into the realm of spiritual life attainment and experience. For example, the Lord once took me through a severe test involving the home in which we lived. Our income had been cut off, and we were unable to pay the rent. The rental agency sent us a registered letter, telling us that we were to move out of the house within a week unless the rent was paid in full.

The time expired and even though we were informed that we would be moved into the street, I clearly felt the Lord saying that we were not to leave. I prayed, *"Lord, if You do not meet us soon, this will become the worst mess anyone has ever seen."* It was an exceedingly impossible situation as there was absolutely no apparent way through. Again, the impression came that we were not to move, but we were to continue to trust the Lord; so I obeyed.

A short time later, the Lord, in a very unusual way, provided the rent, and we were able to stay. Through this experience, I learned that His Word can be trusted and that He is faithful. Now, I experientially knew that I could trust my life in His hands.

Another experience helped me to come into a complete trust in His ability to care for us as a family. I had owned a TV cable system and understood electronic repair work but I felt quite limited as to my abilities in the ministry. Knowing I was responsible for my family, I decided that if I was not successful in ministry, or if the Lord did not provide adequately for us, I could go back into business and earn enough to support my family. So I purchased an expensive tube tester that was in a black alligator-like casing, and put it in the attic of our cottage at the Bible School. Now, if it became necessary, I could get it down and use it to earn enough to cover our needs.

By having it available in the attic, I felt I had a reliable alternative.

Then one day in class, the instructor (*Walter Beuttler*) began to talk about *"little black alligators."* He explained how these little creatures made the nicest pets, but they needed to be fed each day, which meant they would grow. Then he added: *"The problem is, the time will come when they will have become big enough to eat you."*

Immediately, the Lord began to deal with me. I strongly felt that what had been presented about this *alligator* was intended for me. Later, as I was waiting on the Lord, an unusual presence of the Lord came, and He brought to my remembrance the tube tester that I had put in the attic, *"just in case."* The Lord reminded me that it was in a black alligator casing. He showed me that I was *"feeding"* it, because I was relying on it to meet our needs, rather than trusting Him implicitly.

Then He showed me that if I continued to rely upon this tube tester for security, it would begin to grow until it would devour me, in regard to His will for my life. Then, a battle started within me. I had paid a high price for *"my alligator"* and I wanted to keep it. I complained to the Lord, *"It cost all that money; what am I to do?"*

A short time later, during a missionary convention, an urgent need was presented. The Lord began to deal with me to make a pledge, and I resisted because I did not have the money to pay it. Then came the thought of the tube tester, and the Lord asked me if I was willing to give it up. In a few days, a postcard arrived from the man who had purchased my business. He needed a tube tester, had remembered that I had one, and wondered if I might be willing to sell it. I said that I would and was able to pay the missionary pledge I had made.

When necessary, the Lord may press us into a situation in which we *feel* as if we are standing on a gangplank, blindfolded, with our hands tied behind our back and a sword pressing into us to force us to walk off the end, and fall into what appears to be the depths of hopelessness. This *"gangplank"* is often a set of circumstances that has been arranged by the Lord to accomplish something specific within our lives. It may seem to us that it will be the end of everything as we walk off the end of the plank. However, there is a higher purpose for which the Lord permits these things in order to show us His faithfulness, and to teach us to implicitly trust Him. If we are to become His Bride, then He must so work upon us that we learn to become dependent upon Him for everything.

Again and again, the Lord has wonderfully proven Himself to me as being trustworthy. Each time that I have seemingly walked off the end of this *gangplank*, I have landed in His waiting arms. These experiences have accomplished something deep within my being, beyond anything that could have been learned in any other way. I have experienced the outworking of His redemption, and I have both seen and felt the protection of my Heavenly Bridegroom. I have experientially learned that I can trust Him.

One of the greatest blessings we can ever receive is to experience the *faithfulness* of Jesus. Sometimes we may be overly cautious, or afraid, but the Lord will lead us to the place where we are able to put our implicit trust in Him and then rest. This is not easy, because this ability can only be wrought out through experience, upon the *"anvil"* of life. Yet, it can truly be said that if we are willing to completely entrust our lives into His hands, He will bring us through. We must recognize, however, that there is a difference between presumption and obedience. We must know that He is leading us.

Another experience which the Lord used to bring a correction in my walk with Him came while I was a student at Pine Crest Bible Institute in 1960. The Lord prompted me to set aside the weekly income check that I received from the sale of my business, for a purpose which He would make known later. I was being charged room and board for my family, along with tuition for classes; but now I did not have the money to pay these fees, and my school bill began to climb. Before long, I was called into the office and asked for payment. Because I was not at liberty to reveal the reason I was unable to pay, I was then informed that I had to pay the past due amount within ten days or move out. I had enough in the bank to pay this; yet the Lord had told me I was to set this money aside.

A few days later, the Lord began to reveal to me many things about Abraham. He had told Abraham to go <u>up</u> into the land that He would show him. When Abraham arrived, there was a severe famine; yet the Lord had led him there. Abraham, who had not yet experienced the faithfulness of the Lord, left, and went <u>down</u> into Egypt for provision; but during his time there, he became involved in a serious dilemma.

I saw that if Abraham had trusted the "*word*" he had received from the Lord and stayed, the Lord would have caused the very desert to spring up as a table of plenty. The responsibility rested with the Lord because He had told Abraham to go there. Therefore, during the time of famine, his need would have been met. But instead of looking to the Lord, Abraham turned to Egypt, a type of the world system, for provision.

The next day, I learned that a factory in town was hiring; and if I would go, prepared for work, I could start immediately. This seemed right, for I could then approach the president of the school and tell him that I was working and would soon be able to pay the bill. The Lord quickly reminded me of all that He had just shown me about Abraham. Now I realized that I was about to go "*down to Egypt*" to have my need met, rather than trust the Lord. It was not easy to say no, but I had no choice if I was to please the Lord and truly learn to trust Him. I had to wait for His provision.

There were only three days remaining until I would be told to leave. While I was on a ladder, patching some ceiling plaster, the following thoughts ran through my mind. I said within myself, "*In the past when the Lord spoke to me, He always made a way through for me. This is the same voice telling me to set this money aside. If this is truly the Lord, He will make a way.*

*If not, I need to know. So, I will get down from this ladder, and
I will go and tell the school president that I cannot pay the bill.
Then, I will go to my apartment, pack, and leave."*

Then, deep within me, the thought formed, *"Although I do not
understand, I will find a place to live and I will serve the Lord
anyway."* As soon as I expressed this, a very heavy presence of
the Lord came upon me; so much so, that I had to bend over the
top of the ladder to keep from falling off. The Lord spoke again
and said, *"This is what I wanted to hear. Now, go and use the
money to pay your school bill."*

I was very disappointed, as I wanted to go to the president of the
school and tell him that I could not pay. I had thought, *"Perhaps
something spectacular will happen when I tell him I cannot
pay my school bill."* However, I very reluctantly withdrew the
money from the bank and paid the school the amount due.

About two weeks later, I received further understanding
concerning Abraham. The Lord showed me that He had
miraculously given Abraham a son, Isaac, who was the result
of the *"promise"* that had been given to Abraham and Sarah.
Because of the impossible circumstances due to their age, and
the greatness of this miracle, Abraham had come to love Isaac
more than the Lord, and a correction became necessary.

Likewise, the Lord said that I also had received a *promise*. My
promise was that I would come into the possession of a special
"set-apart" place. Previously, while waiting upon the Lord, I
had been caught up and completely engulfed in a visible Glory
which I saw in brilliant color, as I stood before the Throne of
God. During this time, the Lord made known to me, without my
hearing any words, but rather through an understanding that
powerfully came into me through this moving, visible Glory,
that I was to establish a teaching center that would emphasize
our becoming sensitive and responsive to both His voice and
His manifest presence, and also, prepare many for His end-time
intervention purposes.

After learning of His purpose for me, "*my ministry*" began to mean more to me than my times of fellowship with the Lord. Seeking the ministry that He had for me began to occupy so much of my time and energy that I left the place of an abiding communion with the Lord that I had once known. Then I realized that the Lord could not allow me to continue in this way. He said, "*You love your Isaac (this set-apart place) more than Me. Therefore, I led you up on the mount (I was on top of a ladder when all this happened) with your Isaac (promise) to offer him. Then you raised the knife by saying, 'I will tell the president of the school that I cannot pay the bill, and I will pack and leave, but I will serve You anyway.' When I saw that you were ready to slay your promise in obedience, I was then satisfied.*" Once again, the Lord became *first* in my life, as a correction was made.

This was all that He wanted of Abraham. When Abraham raised the knife, Isaac immediately became *second*. Abraham had restored the *first place* in his life to the Lord and He was satisfied. The Lord desires to work out His creative purpose in each of our lives, even though it may *seem* to lead to the end of all that *we* desire. The way into this life of *expectant trust* is by taking up our cross and following Him.

> "...**Except a corn of wheat fall into the ground and die, it abides alone: but if it die, it brings forth much fruit.**"
> John 12:24

The Lord will abide faithful. Many times, this has been made experientially real to me. I could have gone to work and paid my school bill, but the loss would have been eternal.

The Lord may allow circumstances in our lives that appear to be impossible, in order to reveal His faithfulness to us. Then He will be able to bring us to the place where we can, in total *trust*, submit to His time and way of bringing His will to pass. As we are His Bride, the Lord has a right to expect this of us. This is why the Bride said, "*Draw me, we will run after You*" (Song of

Solomon 1:4). To "*run*" suggests a reckless daring, whereby we trust the Lord "*in spite of*" circumstances. No longer should our needs or responsibilities be a hindrance to our obedience to Him. So often, we miss the Lord at this point.

A young man, who was called to serve the Lord, had a very good position with the company for which he worked. The Lord began to prompt him to relocate to a specific city in which he was to begin a ministry. He learned that his company had a branch office there and was willing to transfer him, and also, that the cost of living would be considerably higher. Instead of being obedient, he said, "*I will not go unless they pay me more than I make now.*" I felt the grieving of the Holy Spirit when I heard this. He had not learned to be obedient to the leading of the Lord, or to trust His faithfulness.

The Lord does not accept us on the basis of "*our*" terms. The Scripture says, "*For many be called, but few chosen*" (Matthew 20:16). Or, "*Many are called, but few are willing to pay the price in order to be chosen.*" Being chosen is always based on our obedience in qualifying. This is why the Lord said, "*If any man will come after Me, let him deny himself, and take up his cross and follow Me*" (Matthew 16:24). Notice that the Lord said "*if.*" It is up to us to obey.

Through the progressive decisions that we make in choosing *His ways*, and by our diligently cultivating our relationship with Jesus, His image and likeness becomes formed within our being. This is better understood through the following example.

Tickets to enter the Smithsonian Institute were given to two men. Each knew he was to go there at an appointed time. The first man continued to rejoice over the fact that he had a ticket to get in, and this was all he did. But the second man began to read and study about the things that were there. He spent all of his time in preparation for this trip, so he could get the most out of it. The day came when they arrived and presented their tickets.

They came to what appeared to be a rock. To the first, it had no value or purpose. But to the second, it spoke volumes because he had studied and understood why it was there. There had been an inner preparation in his life which gave it meaning.

Sometimes we sing about our having a mansion *"just over the hilltop"* and we speak about the *"streets of gold."* But unless there is something within us (*spiritual substance*) that gives meaning and purpose to His call for us to be seated together with Him in His throne, and unless we have come into His chambers for times of communion with Him, then all this will be only as the *"stone"* was to the first man - it will have no meaning or apparent value.

"By night on my bed, I sought Him....." Song of Solomon 3:1

He leads us through these *dark* places; but afterward when we come into the *light*, we will discover that we have a deeper understanding of the Lord and of the methods He uses to bring us into a higher realm of spirituality. While I was going through my experience on top of the ladder, the true purpose of Abraham's experience never occurred to me. It was later, while waiting on the Lord that it came before me. Then I understood the experience that I had gone through. This gave me a deeper confidence in the Lord, and it built *spiritual substance* into the very fiber of my being, which strengthened me and imparted to me direction and purpose for my life.

Now I was willing, in obedience to Jesus, to take another step upward on the stairs, beyond that which *seemed* to be reasonable; for I had come to know that I could trust Him in whatever situation that He might place in my path. As the Lord begins to build this confidence within us, He separates us from the *"many"* (*the Daughters of Jerusalem*), and begins to view us as His *"singular"* Bride. Only then will He be able to say to us:

"O My dove, *that are* in the clefts of the rock, in the Secret *places* **of the Stairs....."** Song of Solomon 2:14

Here, we can rest in the *approbation* of His favor, and in the *security* of His protection.

Chapter 12

A TIME FOR BEING SHUT AWAY

"A garden enclosed *is* My sister, *My* spouse; a spring shut up, a fountain sealed. Your plants *are* an orchard of pomegranates, with pleasant fruits; camphor, with spikenard, Spikenard and saffron; calamus and cinnamon, with all trees of frankincense; myrrh and aloes, with all the chief spices." Song of Solomon 4:12-14

Her first testimony had been, *"My Beloved is mine"* (Song of Solomon 2:16). The Lord accepted this and allowed His Bride to have all that she desired. At the same time, He began to draw her to Himself by causing her to notice His interest in her.

All Christians understand that they are to seek the Lord. However, few realize that the Lord actively seeks them. After Adam failed in the Garden of Eden and hid from the presence of the Lord, it was the Lord who came, seeking the one who was hiding from Him.

"And the Lord God called to Adam, and said to him, Where *are* you?" Genesis 3:9

So also in the Song of Solomon, the Lord is again seeking; but this time He is seeking a Bride, and again, He is looking for her response.

"...Behold, He stands behind our wall, He looks forth at the windows, showing Himself through the lattice." Song of Solomon 2:9

When she noticed that Jesus was looking through the "*window*" toward her, longing to be invited into the chamber within her spirit that He had created for fellowship, there arose deep within her a stirring toward Him - she began to intently desire "*Him*" rather than all she had previously sought after. Our spiritual sensitivity will be awakened and our spiritual capacity enlarged, as we respond to His desire to be with us and begin to spend quality time waiting upon Him.

Jesus acknowledged that she has a "*single eye*" that is beginning to look upward toward Him alone, and in a penetrating expression of love, He said to her, "*O My dove*" (Song of Solomon 2:14). Because of her newly acquired *single eye*, He can begin to change her into becoming the Bride that He desires - a Bride who will notice His presence, and, desiring to be with Him, will quickly respond whenever He comes, desiring to be with her. In her first confession she said:

> "...**my mother's children were angry with me; they made me the keeper of the vineyards;** *but* **my own vineyard have I not kept.**" Song of Solomon 1:6

She has been a very dedicated and active worker "*for*" the Lord. Even in the heat of the day while others rested, she worked until she became burned by the sun (*I am black, but comely* - Song of Solomon 1:5). During this time, she was so busy that it did not occur to her that she did not have a personal relationship with Jesus. She did not know His voice or His leadings, as she did only as others told her to do (*They made me the keeper of the vineyards*).

She had been so faithful in doing all that was required of her that her own vineyard had been neglected. When we realize and confess that *something* is missing in our spiritual experience, this confession (*our neglected relationship to Jesus*) will become the "*ground*" upon which the Lord will come to draw us into an active relationship with Himself. It is encouraging to know that He will come to meet us - even in the place of neglect, if we will repent and confess our need to Him.

"For we are His workmanship, created in Christ Jesus to good works, which God has before ordained that we should walk in them." Ephesians 2:10

"My own vineyard have I not kept." This *"vineyard"* is the area in which we live and function. It encompasses all of the people and circumstances in our life experience that are available to the Lord for His use in bringing about our spiritual development and growth (*we are His workmanship — the product that is being formed*). It becomes *"good ground"* (Matthew 13:8) when we place Jesus in full control of all that pertains to us and give Him permission to use all this to accomplish His purposes in and through us. This neglected *"vineyard"* also relates to our devotional life.

"But you, when you pray, enter into your closet, and when you have shut your door, pray to your Father which is in secret; and your Father which sees in secret shall reward you openly." Matthew 6:6

Those who desire the Lord's best should have a special *"place"* that has been *"set apart"* and dedicated for times of fellowship with Him, and then pray for an *"open heaven"* over it. Along with this *"set apart"* place for intimate communion with Jesus, we should submit the total area of our life experience to be an *"open door"* for Him to enter. We can do this by maintaining the *"set"* of our spirit *upward* toward the Lord, no matter where we are, or what we are doing. It is this that encourages and releases Jesus to become active in making us the Bride that He desires.

"...let the Bridegroom go forth of His chamber, and the Bride out of her closet." Joel 2:16

This speaks of our maintaining an active, cooperative relationship with Jesus. He will always use us to minister to the needs of others. However, our times of communion with Him are more important to Him than anything that we could do for Him. Jesus is to always have the first place in our daily life experience.

"Come now therefore, and I will send you to Pharaoh,

119

> **that you may bring forth My people the children of Israel out of Egypt."** Exodus 3:10

Notice that we are beckoned to "*come*" to Jesus first, before we are sent to "*go*" forth. Our ministry will be much more effective and productive when it is the result of, and flows out from, our times of communion with the Lord.

> **"Come, My beloved, let us go forth into the field; let us lodge in the villages. Let us get up early to the vineyards; let us see if the vine flourish,** *whether* **the tender grape appear,** *and* **the pomegranates bud forth: <u>there will I give you My loves.</u>"** Song of Solomon 7:11-12

Many servants of the Lord who fail, or get into serious problems, do so because of negligence at this very point - *they work so hard for the Lord that they become spiritually weakened and succumb to temptation.* This happened to the Bride. Thus, she confessed her failure - *"My mother's children were angry with me"* (Song of Solomon 1:6). Our seeking to please others accomplishes little. But when we please the Lord, His approbation (*divine favor*) will rest upon us, and also, upon all that we do.

She had neglected her times of communion with Jesus through being busy, diligently working *for* Him. It is extremely important that we maintain quality times of worship, prayer, waiting upon the Lord, and devotionally reading the Word. We must keep in mind that our ability to impart spiritual life (*the very substance of His being*) to others, results from that which we have *first* received.

Our primary calling is to work *with* the Lord, rather than *for* Him.

> **"And He goes up into a mountain, and calls** *to Him* **whom He would: and they came to Him. And He ordained twelve, that they should be with Him, and that He might send them forth...."** Mark 3:13-14

I learned a principle many years ago that greatly affected my life:

"If we will build God a house of devotion, He will build us a house of ministry." If we are faithful in our part, which is *"being with Him,"* then He will be faithful in His part, to *"send us forth."*

During 1961, I had been spending much time waiting on the Lord. I was prompted to go to a Bible Institute where I had never been. While there, the academic dean prophesied that I had been sent there by the Lord to be a teacher. As a result I was hired and experienced a very successful time of ministry.

"That I may cause those that love Me to inherit substance; and I will fill their treasures." Proverbs 8:21

Any expression of *ministry* that we may have will flow out from the spiritual *"substance"* that we receive from Jesus, as we commune with Him. These *"treasures"* are the deposit of His life within us, so that *"spirit and life"* will flow out (*impartation*) to others through our relationship to Him.

The Bride asked the Lord to *"stay me with flagons, comfort me with apples"* (Song of Solomon 2:5). In response to her desire, He brought her to the banqueting table and blessed her so abundantly with all she wanted, that she became filled beyond her spiritual capacity at that time. She was given more than she could assimilate (*receive*) into her spirit.

"...for I *am* **sick of love."** Song of Solomon 2:5

We are to enjoy the blessings and use to the fullest all the giftings that the Lord has given. Yet, these are not meant to be our goal. Rather, they are to be the means of enlarging our spirit as we minister to the needs of others. Our goal should always be to better know and glorify our Lord.

Outwardly, the Bride seemed to be content. However, the Lord knew that she could not continue to be satisfied and fulfilled by just working for Him, or in having all of the blessings that she desired. She had seen Jesus longingly seek entrance into her life and was moved toward Him. Now He is ready to show her that there is something "*better*" that He desires for her.

He is waiting for her to invite Him to come within the secret place (*the "deep" within her*) to commune with Him, alone. To accomplish this, He allowed her to enter into (*experience*) a time of spiritual darkness.

> **"By night on my bed I sought Him whom my soul loves....**" Song of Solomon 3:1

During this time of darkness, she realized that seeking His blessings and provision alone had not satisfied her, and she frantically began to search for Him.

> **"I will rise now, and go about the city in the streets, and in the broad ways I will seek Him whom my soul loves....**" Song of Solomon 3:2

During this time of searching, she began to understand how incomplete she had been without Him. By the time she found Him, a real change had taken place within her. She is now able to say:

> **"***It was* **but a little that I passed from them** (*all the things she once sought after*)**, but I found Him, whom my soul loves: I held Him and would not let Him go....**"
> Song of Solomon 3:4 (comment added)

The Lord expresses this same spiritual principle to the Laodicean Church.

> **"Because you say, I am rich, and increased with goods, and have need of nothing; and know not that you are wretched, and miserable, and poor, and blind, and naked: I counsel you to buy of Me gold tried in the fire, that you may be rich....**" Revelation 3:17-18

The Laodicean's sought after and were satisfied with, possessions (*rich and increased with goods*). Therefore, the Lord spoke to them concerning their true need, *"gold tried in the fire."* Gold speaks of the divine nature, His image and likeness being wrought out within our spirit. We will become like Him as we spend quality time with Him.

Now, the Lord is ready to take her a step further. In order to make a deep and lasting impression within her, concerning Himself, He brought before her a glorious revelation of His person and presence, as He came forth from the wilderness clothed in all of His manifest glory and sovereign power.

> **"Who *is* this that comes out of the wilderness like pillars of smoke, perfumed with myrrh and frankincense, with all powders of the merchant? Behold His bed, which *is* Solomon's; threescore valiant men *are* about it, of the valiant of Israel."** Song of Solomon 3:6-7

It is essential for each one of us to come to the place where we personally, implicitly, can trust both our Lord's willingness, and His ability, to keep us during our wilderness experience, or during any time of difficulty we face, and then safely bring us out.

Immediately after the excitement and glory of this experience, the Lord made an arrangement in which she became as a *"garden enclosed"* (Song of Solomon 4:12). Here, she will be separated for a time, from all material influences and outside activities, to the Lord Himself. During this time of *"separation"* within the garden, all that she had come to know *"about"* the Lord will become a personalized *"reality"* within her, as she spends time <u>alone</u> waiting upon Him in His presence.

Then, in His time and way, that which she *"becomes"* while within the garden will find its full expression and outworking, as she daily walks out His will and purpose for her life. She is about to experience what the Lord meant when He said:

> **"...buy of Me gold tried in the fire...."** Revelation 3:18

This *"garden enclosed"* is designed to bring forth the very best of the potential that the Lord has seen to be within her (*us*). Although it is situated in a very beautiful setting, it represents a realm of intense "*personal dealings*," so she hesitated to enter. The Lord knew she would attempt to leave before He could fully accomplish within her all that He desired. Therefore, He built a high wall around the garden, making it completely "*enclosed*," so she would not be able to leave. The Lord is able to keep us where He has placed us.

> **"A garden enclosed *is* My sister, *My* spouse; a spring shut up, a fountain sealed."** Song of Solomon 4:12

This high wall also hindered all, *except the Lord*, from entering. It separated her from the fellowship of her friends and from all those who would attempt to occupy her time or divert her to a lesser realm of spiritual experience. Also, during this set-apart time, her "*giftings*" failed to operate and her enabling for "*ministry*" was cut off. She is now separated from all that she has been accustomed to and dependent upon. She has become a "*garden enclosed*," separated to the Lord, Himself.

The nine plants mentioned as being in this garden are types of the nine-fold fruit of the Spirit. They represent the "*quality*" of spirit that the Lord desires to develop within her (*us*) during this time of separation.

> **"Your plants *are* an orchard of pomegranates, with pleasant fruits: camphire, with spikenard, Spikenard and saffron; calamus and cinnamon, with all trees of frankincense: myrrh and aloes, with all the chief spices."** Song of Solomon 4:13-14

The "*orchard... with pleasant fruits*" within the garden, speaks of the spiritual maturity that is unfolding within her, a display of righteousness, peace, and joy, as she grows in spiritual understanding and wisdom.

During this time of being set apart, there were times when she had a desire for expression, or ministry: *"If I could just get out and share all that I am receiving."* But the Lord had made her *"a garden enclosed."*

Through being shut in by the Lord *for a season*, she became much more *sensitive* in her ability to recognize His voice and His presence; thus, she was able to respond more promptly to His desire for her fellowship.

> **"...for You have created all things, and for Your pleasure they are and were created."** Revelation 4:11

We were created for His pleasure. Therefore, there are times when the Lord desires to be personally alone with us (*I will come into him*), that He might sup with us and then, we with Him.

> **"Behold, I stand at the door, and knock: if any man hear My voice, and open the door, I will come in to him, and will sup with him, and he with Me."** Revelation 3:20

As we spiritually mature, past seeking for ourselves, these times of *"supping"* will lead us into the experience of the *"fellowship of His sufferings"* in which Jesus shares His burdens with us.

> **"That I may know Him, and the power of His resurrection, and the fellowship of His sufferings, being made conformable to His death."** Philippians 3:10

There are different *"levels"* of separation. There are those who are called primarily to a ministry of intercession. Being an intercessor requires much more from us than our times of prayer. It involves our becoming identified with, *or pregnant with*, the problem or need of another, in order to pray it through. Intercession is born of the Spirit and operates through inner travail. It means getting alone and wrestling with a burden until it is birthed through the agony of birth pains.

A ministry of intercession produces far greater results than most may realize. There are those who are called to this hidden ministry of intercession who are not known to man, but only to the Lord. They have become as "*a garden enclosed*" to Him. Vocal travail in intercession, which is essential to this ministry, should, as much as possible, be done apart from others.

There are *others* who are shut in with the Lord in "*hidden*" ministries. These primarily minister only to the Lord, but He may arrange for certain "*daughters of Jerusalem*" to *notice* the evident favor of God that rests upon them, and *seek* their help in coming into a higher level of spiritual life and experience.

In an unusual way, my path crossed the lives of two men, (*John W. Follette and Walter Beuttler*), who lived on this level of separation to the Lord Himself, but were willing to be used in this type of "*hidden*" ministry. Therefore, they had a vital part in the forming of my spiritual life.

During times when I was going through some very intense struggles, their intercession, prayers, and words of wisdom, as well as my being challenged by what I observed them to be spiritually, enabled me to partake of this higher realm of spiritual life. Through the impact of their lives upon my spirit, the very "*substance*" of God was imparted into the inner depths of my being.

There is much responsibility and reward in a hidden ministry of this type. The Lord is looking for those who will stand between Him and the need, and then *travail* until He is able to move upon the situation to accomplish His purpose.

There are *a few* whom the Lord leads into this "*garden enclosed*" to remain there. Some of the Lord's choicest saints have been separated from all spiritual activity, and are enclosed within this garden that He might come to them as He desires to enjoy uninterrupted times of fellowship and communion with them.

The extravagance that our Lord expresses in the vastness of His creation (*the universe*) is evident, as we enjoy the manifold multicolored flowers of spring and the rich brilliance of color in the departing leaves of fall. So also, the Lord can afford the luxury of being extravagant in setting aside *"whom He will"* for His purposes and glory.

As the Lord entered the Garden of Eden to walk with Adam, so also, He comes into this *"garden enclosed"* to commune with His Bride (*us*). Thus, within this *"garden enclosed"* are those who are so completely given to the Lord, that they are known to Him alone.

Most of those whom the Lord draws into this garden are intended to stay only for a limited time. He leads them back out again to become a *"witness"* of all that they received while in His chambers - *alone with Him whom they intensely love.* They reluctantly leave His presence to minister to those who desire more of the Lord, but are not yet ready to be drawn into this garden experience. As these pick *"fruit"* from the lives of those who have been within, they also will be drawn to enter.

"And they heard the voice of the Lord God walking in the garden in the cool of the day...." Genesis 3:8

Here, as she basks in the glow and warmth of His presence, she prays (*as we also should pray*) that the wind (*Holy Spirit*) would come and blow upon her garden. She desires that the inward beauty, which is developing as she basks in His presence, will become as a beautiful fragrance (*spices*) that will flow out from her to bring pleasure and satisfaction to the One she has come to intimately love.

"Awake, O north wind; and come, you south; blow upon my garden, *that* **the spices thereof may flow out...."** Song of Solomon 4:16

Rather than seeking to receive a word or blessing from the Lord for herself, she desires that she herself might become a blessing (*the spices flowing out*) and give back to Him, *with increase,* from all that He has imparted into her being.

127

"...I am come that they might have life, and that they might have *it* more abundantly." John 10:10

This *"wind"* is a type of the *lifting* power of the Holy Spirit, which draws us upward from the earthly into the realms of the spiritual. When Nicodemus came to Jesus, he asked if entering the Kingdom of God was comparable to reentering the *"womb."* Jesus responded by likening it instead to the *"wind."* He said:

"The wind blows where it lists, and you hear the sound thereof, but can not tell from where it comes, and to where it goes...." John 3:8

"The wind blows where He pleases." This reveals that we can neither understand that which is spiritual, nor enter the realms of the Spirit through any mental or physical means, but only by means of spiritual perception and enabling. Then He added:

"...so is every one that is born of the Spirit." John 3:8

The *"wind"* speaks of *"divine activity"* which *"lifts"* us into the realms of the spiritual. The *"north wind"* brings *"correction"* to our walk in order to lift us above all that is earthly. The *"south wind"* gives *"direction"* to our walk and establishes us in the heavenlies. This twofold working of the wind brings first (*north wind*), the *"chastening"* work of the Holy Spirit, along with corrective teaching; and second (*south wind*), an active relationship with our Heavenly Bridegroom as we commune with Him. The desire of the Lord is to lift us above our self-seeking desires, as quickly and painlessly as possible.

When the Bride prays, *"Awake, O north wind,"* she not only is giving the Holy Spirit permission, but also is encouraging Him to bring about the needed changes within her. As He communes with her, she longs to be set free and delivered from every aspect of her self-life so she can be brought into alignment with His desire for an active, ongoing involvement with her in the outworking of His purposes. Whatever the cost might be, she now desires to flow in harmony with Him, as now she *feels* the touch of His presence.

The Lord's chastening hand upon our lives is truly a blessing, when we understand the purpose for it; for He chastens those whom He loves.

"For whom the Lord loves He chastens....**"** Hebrews 12:6

Now she is able to ask with confidence, and respond to His correcting hand as it is applied to her life experience.

"Awake, O north wind; and come... **blow upon my garden**....**"** Song of Solomon 4:16

As the Holy Spirit worked within her in answer to her prayer, she became aware of an increase in her desire to be with Him, and also, she felt an increased awareness of His desire to be with her. Now, she understood that the purpose of the *"north wind"* was to *change* her so she could become a Bride who would truly please the Bridegroom (*Jesus*). This caused worship and thanksgiving to rise up from within her, and flow out to Him.

"...and come, you south; blow upon my garden, *that* **the spices thereof may flow out. Let my Beloved come into His garden and eat His pleasant fruits."** Song of Solomon 4:16

As she rightly responded to the *"north wind"* and felt the warmth and comfort of the *"south wind,"* she was able to enter a place of rest in His presence: she knew (*spiritual perception*) that her response was pleasing to Him and that He would do what was right in her behalf.

There is a *"lifting"* aspect within the presence of the Lord. As we respond to His presence, we will begin to flow with it, as being *lifted* by the wind (*a wheel in the middle of a wheel*). As we continue to wait in His presence, we will be quickened by the Holy Spirit and empowered to move with Him, as He leads (*they turned not when they went*).

"The appearance of the wheels and their work *was* **like to the color of a beryl: and they four had one likeness: and their appearance and their work** *was* **as it were a wheel in the middle of a wheel. When they went, they went upon their four sides:** *and* **they turned not when they went."** Ezekiel 1:16-17

As we begin to function in a *cooperative* relationship with Jesus, as being a *"wheel in the middle of a wheel,"* our understanding of this higher *realm* of divine activity and relationship will be confirmed through a further unfolding of His Word, which will cause us to more deeply love and trust Him. It is important for us to understand that all spiritual experiences must agree with the written Word of God.

As these north and south winds each had their intended effect upon the Bride and accomplished their purpose within her, she cried out:

"...Let my Beloved come into His garden and eat His pleasant fruits." Song of Solomon 4:16

He quickly responded to this and said:

"I am come into My garden...." Song of Solomon 5:1

This speaks of His *"manifest presence."* The Lord is omnipresent; that is, He is everywhere as He *"fills"* heaven and earth.

"Can any hide himself in secret places that I shall not see him? says the Lord. Do not I fill heaven and earth? says the Lord." Jeremiah 23:24

The *manifest* presence of the Lord transcends the *omnipresence* of the Lord. The word *"manifest"* means that His presence becomes localized and consciously apparent to one or more of our five physical senses, such as our *"smelling"* the fragrance of His presence.

Through His *"omnipresence,"* we are made aware of the sovereign power of God and receive a sense of divine presence. Through His *"manifest presence,"* the Lord comes to us in such a way that we not only sense His nearness and power, but also we are made consciously aware of Him as being a person who has thoughts and feelings. It is here that we enter with Him into *"the fellowship of His sufferings"* (Philippians 3:10).

> **"...If any man hear My voice, and open the door** (*the point of transition from His omnipresence into His manifest presence*), **I will come in to him, and sup with him, and he with Me."** Revelation 3:20 (comment added)

This *"supping"* is an intimate, personal exchange. Thus, the Lord comes to us in this intimate and personal way to share His feelings and thoughts with us, and to partake of the *"substance"* we have received from Him. His partaking of us (*I have eaten My honeycomb with My honey*) is a divine mystery.

> **"I am come into My garden, My sister, *My* spouse: I have gathered My myrrh with My spice; I have eaten My honeycomb with My honey...."** Song of Solomon 5:1

Then He adds:

> **"...eat, O friends; drink, yea, drink abundantly, O beloved."** Song of Solomon 5:1

Notice that there is an *"exchange."* The Lord will cause others (*eat, O friends*) to come and partake of all that we receive, as we partake (*drink abundantly*) of Him. Paul understood this principle and applied it to his ministry.

> **"For we which live are always delivered to death for Jesus' sake, that the life also of Jesus might be made manifest in our mortal flesh. So then death works in us, but life in you."** II Corinthians 4:11-12

Paul ministered his very life to others. All true ministry includes an *impartation* of the spiritual substance of our relationship to the Lord, along with the anointed Word that we minister. Many (*eat, O friends*) come to "*feed*" upon those who have this quality of spiritual substance within them, and then go away leaving them drained. This is especially true of those who are heavily *anointed* and have a ministry of *impartation*. Thus, ministry works death in the one who is giving, but life in all those who receive.

Therefore, after a time of giving out in ministry, we must come back to the source of all life, our Lord Jesus Christ, and again partake of His life in order to regain that which has been given (*imparted*) to others. Jesus said:

> "...**Except you eat the flesh of the Son of Man, and drink His blood, you have no life in you.**" John 6:53

The Lord comes to fellowship with us, and also, to strengthen and change us while we are alone with Him in this "*garden enclosed.*" Here, as He shares Himself with us, He is released to draw into our path those who are presently not able to come into this place of intimate communion with Him. We feed on the Lord, *then others come to feed on us*, thereby receiving His life through us.

This places a great responsibility upon each of us, that the "*true source*" of our spiritual life is Jesus, and that the intention and purpose of the impartation that flows out through us is pure. As others partake of our spiritual life and experiences, a spiritual capacity will be created within them. As this partaking continues, the Lord will cause them to realize that there is something better than continuing to be satisfied with only "*feeding*" on the experiences of another. Thus, they will begin to look for the Lord Himself, and say to Him, as we once did:

> "**Tell me, O You whom my soul loves, where You feed, where You make** *Your flock* **to rest at noon: for why should I be as one that turns aside by the flocks of Your companions?**" Song of Solomon 1:7

The Lord answered and said:

"If you know not... go your way forth by the footsteps of the flock...." Song of Solomon 1:8

In other words, the Lord is telling them to find one who knows and has experienced the way. It is very important at this point, that we ourselves have personally experienced and know the way. Only then will we be able to lead those who are seeking *something more,* to the Lord Himself.

Because we have been spending time with Jesus and have learned to sup with Him, many will be enabled to come into a deeper relationship with Jesus and experience the reality of personally knowing Him. We must be careful that those who receive from our ministry are directed to Jesus, not drawn to us.

Through our times of communion and prayer, as we continue to sup with Jesus, we will receive much spiritual *"substance"* into our being. Notice that the Lord gladly tells others to come and feed upon our spiritual life and experience because we have fed on Him. It is a profound and marvelous compliment when the Lord is able to say this about us, for we have become:

"A fountain of gardens, a well of living waters, and streams from Lebanon." Song of Solomon 4:15

Chapter 13

SHUT IN WITH HIM ALONE

"A garden enclosed *is* My sister, *My* spouse; a spring shut up, a fountain sealed." Song of Solomon 4:12

The Bride has come to the place in her spiritual experience where she is able to view the Bridegroom (*Jesus*) with a *"single eye"* and respond to Him as He leads or indicates. She has progressed in her relationship with Him to the extent that she is no longer content with simply being blessed, apart from His presence. She longs to be with Him.

To bring about this change, the Lord prepared a special *"garden enclosed"* where she became as a *"spring shut up, a fountain sealed."* Here, she was alone, separated from all that she had known in her past experiences. Her spiritual giftings and abilities seemed to dry up, causing her to feel spiritually dead. Yet at the same time, she became aware of her need to personally know Jesus and to abide in His presence.

At this very critical moment, while she was feeling this intense desire for His presence, the Lord came within the Garden and revealed Himself to her as a Bridegroom who greatly desires to be with His Bride. Here, shut in alone with Him, she experienced a very satisfying time of fellowship with Him. She discovered that she is enjoying His presence much more now, than in the past when she was occupied with seeking the blessings and gifts that

He was able to give. Now, with a single eye, she longs to be with Him. She has become very sensitive to His feelings and desires.

This *"garden enclosed"* is a special *atmosphere* that is created through a *divine arrangement* for those who have come to the place in their spiritual experience where they desire, above all else, the Lord Himself. Here, in this *set-apart* environment, the Lord will cause us to *"rest,"* while He *"works"* deep within us, to change us into that which He has seen us to be (*our spiritual potential*).

"I have compared you, O My love, to a company of horses in Pharaoh's chariots." Song of Solomon 1:9

We are to simply *"abide"* within the confines of this *garden enclosed* and respond in heart obedience as He directs. Now we are ready to follow, as He leads.

"And have <u>made us</u> to our God kings and priests: and we shall reign on the earth." Revelation 5:10

Here, as we spend time *"waiting upon the Lord"* in expectancy, He will energize from deep within us the spiritual qualities which, although buried and inactive, had attracted His attention to us. Now, as our life begins to more perfectly reflect His life, these abiding spiritual qualities will surface and attract others to the Lord.

"I love them that love Me; and those that seek Me early shall find Me." Proverbs 8:17

"Those" who truly love the Lord and have cultivated a sensitivity to His presence, will come often into this *"set-apart"* place (*closet*) to commune with Him (*seek Me early*). This will cause the Lord to become singularly interested in *"them that love Me."*

As we intently express to Jesus our love for Him, He will create an enlarged spiritual hunger within us. This inner heart cry will find its expression as a prayer, *"Draw me,"* which He longs to hear and answer. His response to the expression of our love for

Him will provoke us to seek Him even more. This will result in our willingness to make an unqualified commitment to Him; *"we will run after You."* Together these culminate in a beautiful and satisfying *"garden"* experience in which we can testify, *"The King has brought me into His chambers"* (Song of Solomon 1:4).

Just as the Lord created the *"Garden of Eden"* for Adam and Eve, He will also prepare a *"set apart place"* for those of us who are willing to sincerely pray this prayer of desire to intimately know Him. As we obediently *"respond"* to whatever amount of spiritual hunger He has placed within us, and as we begin to *"run"* after Him, He will reveal to us the *"secret"* of climbing the stairs (*many levels of experience*) that lead upward into the chamber (*room*) of His intimate presence.

It is not how much spiritual hunger we have, rather, it is what we do with the hunger that we have, no matter how limited it may be, that touches the heart of the Lord in our behalf.

While the Bride was experiencing *"joy unspeakable"* (*being alone with Him in the garden*), she asked the Holy Spirit to quicken her, that her life might more fully bring pleasure and satisfaction to her Heavenly Bridegroom, the Lord Jesus Christ, and then, *together with Him*, to others.

> **"Awake, O north wind; and come, you south; blow upon my garden,** *that* **the spices thereof may flow out...."** Song of Solomon 4:16

To pray *"Awake, O north wind... and blow upon my garden"* is extremely important and necessary for those who desire something beyond their present spiritual attainment. This is our invitation to the Holy Spirit to develop within us the quality and beauty that will not only please the Lord, but will also prepare us to become a witness of Him to others.

Her second request in this prayer, *"come, you south; blow upon my garden,"* also has a special part in our spiritual development.

This speaks of the Holy Spirit anointing us, so that the spiritual beauty that has developed within us will radiate out from us as an expression of worship and love, bringing pleasure to our Heavenly Bridegroom. As He receives this expression of our love, His "*approbation*" will begin to rest upon us.

"O taste and see that the Lord *is* good: blessed *is* the man *that* trusts in Him." Psalm 34:8

This "*witness*" (*taste and see*) means that our life is reflecting His life to others. We are providing them with a "*taste*" of the satisfying love relationship that has developed between us and the Bridegroom, which will stir them to also seek Him.

This prayer for the "*north wind*" (*His dealings*) to blow upon our garden will find its full outworking in our lives *only* as we unconditionally submit our will, and all of our circumstances, to the Lord. In asking this, we are not only giving Him permission, but encouraging Him to freely work within us to accomplish all that He desires. When we do this, He will respond and begin to work at the root of each hindering problem that we have, in order to bring us into the intimate relationship with Him that He desires.

The result will be an abiding *divine presence and anointing* (*the south wind*) that will bring forth from within us an expression of the beauty of our Heavenly Bridegroom, and enable us to be more responsive and available to Him. Others will sense the warmth and glow of this "*south wind*" flowing out from us.

"...Let my Beloved come into His garden, and eat His pleasant fruits." Song of Solomon 4:16

The changes that have taken place within her, from "*self-centered getting*" to "*Christ-centered giving*" so please her, that she now invites the Lord to abide in the very center of all that she is and does, for His satisfaction and purposes. This is a complete reversal from her past desires and requests, which concerned only what He had to give. Now, she can say with David:

"One *thing* have I desired of the Lord, that will I seek after; that I may dwell in the house of the Lord all the days of my life, to behold the beauty of the Lord, and to inquire in His temple." Psalm 27:4

No longer is she satisfied with only being a *"keeper of the vineyard"* for the benefit of her mother's children (Song of Solomon 1:6). She feels free to ask entrance into His chambers, that she might have a part with Him in all that He seeks to accomplish.

"Tell me, O You whom my soul loves, where You feed...?" Song of Solomon 1:7

He had been patiently waiting to hear this and quickly responded:

"I am come into My garden, My sister, *My* spouse...." Song of Solomon 5:1

The Lord greatly desires to come and fellowship with us. During this time of quiet fellowship with her in the Garden, He found many things within her life that pleased and satisfied Him.

"...I have gathered My myrrh with My spice; I have eaten My honeycomb with My honey; I have drunk My wine with My milk...." Song of Solomon 5:1

When *"God created man in His own image"* (Genesis 1:27), He placed within each of us the ability to recognize His voice and respond to His presence.

"Deep calls to deep...." Psalm 42:7

By divine arrangement, there is a created *"deep"* within each of us that is capable of responding to this *"deep"* call from our Creator. The *"deep"* within us is a *"garden"* in which we can establish an *"environment"* (*a set apart place*) in which this desire of our Creator to commune and fellowship with us can find its fulfillment. Therefore, we should thoughtfully set apart and dedicate a special place where we can turn aside to meet with Him, alone. Jesus confirmed this when He said that we are to go into our *"closet"* and shut the door, and there, in secret, pray to our Father.

"But you, when you pray, enter into your closet, and when you have shut your door, pray to your Father which is in secret; and your Father which sees in secret shall reward you openly." Matthew 6:6

The first picture that we are given of the outworking of this created spiritual capacity which the Lord has placed within each of us is seen in the Garden of Eden. The Lord came at specific times, *"in the cool of the evening,"* and walked (*communed*) with Adam. The Lord also has placed within the pattern of each of our lives a *"cool of the evening."*

There is within the *"makeup"* of each of us, a *"unique time"* during which we can best meet the Lord. For some, it may be early in the morning. Others can best commune with Him late in the evening. It is very important that we seek out and identify this special time, and set it apart for fellowship with Him. He will notice our doing this and will respond to our desire to walk with Him, as He walked with Adam.

First, there was her *"step of obedience"* in being willing to be shut away from everything to which she had become accustomed, in order to become *"a garden enclosed"* to Him. She was so completely changed during her time of separation in the garden that now, she longs for Him alone. Her eye has truly become single toward Him.

The *"garden enclosed"* that she became has now become *"His garden."* In anticipation of His times of communion and fellowship with her, He is able to say with an expression of joy:

"I am come into My garden, My sister, *My* spouse...."
Song of Solomon 5:1

His approbation, or singular love is resting upon her life and she has become attentive to it. He can freely come to her, knowing that she will respond with anticipation to His desire to commune with her in His chambers, or to walk with her in the vineyard for the outworking of His purposes.

> **"Come, My beloved... Let us get up early to the vineyards... there will I give you My loves."**
> Song of Solomon 7:11, 12

Chapter 14

THE TEST OF OBEDIENCE

"Behold, I stand at the door, and knock: if any man hear My voice, and open the door, I will come in to him, and will sup with him, and he with Me." Revelation 3:20

If we have within us an established determination to come apart often to *"wait upon"* the Lord, the fact that Jesus will come and knock on the door of our heart is certain. As we *"wait for"* Him in expectancy, He may simply come to fellowship with us, or He may choose to accomplish something either within, or through us during this time. Our part is to stay in His presence until we feel released.

Also, He may come at times other than those that we choose, which may not be convenient for us. Nevertheless, He desires a prompt, unquestioning response from us.

"If any man hear... and open." The word *"if"* tells us that the Lord's coming into the *"chamber of our spirit"* to commune with us is conditional. We are given the option either to ignore His approaches, or to respond and invite Him to come within. Our *"prompt obedience"* in response to His knocking, will open the door that leads into His presence.

Since He may knock on the door of our spirit at a time that is unexpected or even inconvenient, it is very important that we maintain the *upward poise (sensitivity)* of our spirit so we can hear and respond to His knock, even when we are busy, or at work. This "*knock*" upon the door that leads into the chamber of our spirit can be heard in many ways, which we gradually will learn to recognize. Even our misses will help us in learning His voice, if we are careful to not condemn ourselves.

> **"I love them that love Me; and those that seek Me early** (*respond promptly*) **shall find Me."** Proverbs 8:17 (comment added)

The Lord's approach to us may come in many different forms or ways. The "*ability*" to hear and rightly respond to His "*knocking*" can be cultivated. It is both possible and desirable that we continually "*listen*" (*maintain our spiritual sensitivity*), so we will be available, should the Lord desire our fellowship and come to make His presence known to us. This can be done even during times when we are busy, or at work.

This passage of Scripture also expresses a condition. This "*early*" relates to our responding quickly to His seeking presence. To successfully maintain the ability to hear His voice, we must establish deep within us a "*pre-disposition*" that we will listen, respond, and obey, no matter what we may be involved in at that time.

> **"The secret of the Lord** *is* **with them that fear Him** (*a reverence that results in unquestioning trust and obedience*)**; and He will show them His covenant."** Psalm 25:14 (comment added)

Our Lord is searching for a Bride who is prepared and willing to respond to His presence whenever He may choose to come. As she withdraws from secular activity and invites Him to enter the "*room*" (*chamber*) of her spirit, He will reciprocate by sharing with her His burden concerning His vineyard. To these, He is able to say:

> **"Come, My beloved, let us go forth into the field; let us lodge in the villages. Let us get up early to the vineyards; let us see if the vine flourish,** *whether* **the tender grape appear,** *and* **the pomegranates bud forth: there will I give you My loves."** Song of Solomon 7:11-12

"Come, My beloved, let us go forth..." Many place the emphasis on *"let us go forth."* However, she must first *"come"* to Him. Then together, they will be able to *"go."* This foundational principle, when rightly understood, will strengthen our relationship with the Lord and lead us toward spiritual maturity. As we respond to His call to *"come"* and *"turn aside"* for times of fellowship, He will share His secrets and burdens with us. This is the *"heart"* of our partaking with Jesus in the *"fellowship of His sufferings"* (Philippians 3:10).

Also, it is during these times of intimate fellowship and communion that He imparts His very life (*divine substance*) into us, that His life might be seen through our lives. Only then will we be ready to work *"with"* Him in ministry, rather than our simply working *"for"* Him.

Throughout the Song of Songs, we should be encouraged by the fact that the Bridegroom, due to His intense desire to be with His Bride, came again and again seeking fellowship with her. We can also learn from the problems that resulted due to the reluctance of the Bride to respond to the Bridegroom's approaches, especially when He returned to knock upon the door of her heart at inconvenient times.

The necessary steps in the development of the Bride's capacity to recognize His presence, and the corrective dealings to produce the motivation and understanding to enable her to promptly respond to His presence at any time, are clearly set forth within the Song of Solomon. As we observe her mistakes and consider the methods that the Lord uses to bring about the necessary corrections, we will be helped in our ability to rightly respond to His presence, as He seeks our fellowship.

After a time of fellowship with His Bride in the *"garden enclosed,"* the Bridegroom withdrew His presence and left her there, alone. During their times of intimate communion, Jesus received from her that which was very meaningful to Him. Therefore, He desired to develop an even closer relationship with her. This is better understood by considering the following verse:

> **"...I have gathered My myrrh with My spice; I have eaten My honeycomb with My honey; I have drunk My wine with My milk...."** Song of Solomon 5:1

Jesus came to partake of the *quality* of her spiritual life. After His departure, the Bride, feeling a deep sense of satisfaction, peace, and rest, quietly pondered all that the Bridegroom had spoken, along with all that had been accomplished within her during their time together.

While basking in the lingering effect of His presence, she recognized that her spirit had been both quickened and fed, while she was with Him. She was becoming sensitive to the realm of the Spirit, and as a result, desired more.

> **"I sleep, but my heart wakes...."** Song of Solomon 5:2

As she rested upon her bed, she continued to meditate on this blessed time of communion with the Bridegroom, within the *"garden"* of her spirit. Suddenly, she faintly heard His voice, again desiring her fellowship.

> **"...***It is* **the voice of my Beloved that knocks,** *saying,* **Open to Me, My sister, My love, My dove, My undefiled...."** Song of Solomon 5:2

She heard Him knock, but responded with an excuse:

> **"I have put off my coat; how shall I put it on? I have washed my feet; how shall I defile them?"** Song of Solomon 5:3

She acknowledged His desire to be with her, but she was not willing to be inconvenienced by responding to Him. She was satisfied and comfortable as she rested upon her bed, content with the memory of their past visit, and she desired nothing further from Him. She was satisfied with the memory of what had been.

146

Notice that she heard His knock and that her spirit was willing to respond: *"My heart wakes."* But her flesh was weak, and she was not inclined to be disturbed: *"I sleep."* There was still much that needed to be accomplished within her in order to bring about the changes that would enable her to become the Bride that Jesus desires.

"Jesus answered and said to him, If a man love Me, he will keep My words: and My Father will love him, and We will come to him, and make Our abode with him." John 14:23

He must have a Bride who will obediently welcome Him whenever He comes to invite her to participate with Him in the outworking of His purposes.

"Come, My beloved, let us go forth into the field...." Song of Solomon 7:11

First, we acknowledge and respond to His presence, and then, in a spirit of total cooperation and anticipation, accompany Jesus wherever He may desire to go. The fact that it is Jesus who is both knocking and actively desiring fellowship with His Bride, reveals the other side of our seeking Him. This depicts our Lord as a seeking God who aggressively longs to be with us (*We will come... and make Our abode with him*).

God created man in His own likeness, with the ability to know His voice and the capacity for intelligent, satisfying communion with Him. David spoke of the seeking heart of the Lord in Psalm 42:7:

"Deep calls to deep...."

There is a *"deep"* within the very depths of God that desires fellowship with man. Therefore, He created within man the same depth of spirit, a capacity for communion to which He could relate that He might find the fellowship and satisfaction that He desires. Throughout the Scriptures, the Lord is revealed as a seeking God.

"For the eyes of the Lord run to and fro throughout the whole earth, to show Himself strong in the behalf of *them* **whose heart** *is* **perfect toward Him...."** II Chronicles 16:9

"For the eyes of the Lord *are* **over the righteous, and His ears** *are open* **to their prayers...."** I Peter 3:12

At times, we may feel that the Lord does not notice us, or perhaps, is not interested in us. However, He is far more interested in us, and in revealing and making Himself known to us, than we are in having Him do so. The Lord intensely desires to bring us into an *abiding* experience of communion and fellowship with Him, that we might become *"one"* with Him. He longs to draw us apart to Himself within His chambers, where He can reveal to us an understanding of His ways, and also, of His coming Kingdom.

A teacher (*Walter Beuttler*) in the Bible School I attended gave this example of the seeking heart of the Lord and how He apprehends us. The school had a long, winding lane that led out to the highway. There were tall evergreen trees on both sides, which were so thick that it was difficult for light to penetrate through them at night.

One evening, he was walking with his young daughter, holding her hand as it was so dark that they were unable to see one another. As they walked, he suddenly let loose of her hand and stepped back. He could vaguely see her outline and had to concentrate on her form so as not to lose sight of her. When she realized that he was gone and she was in the darkness alone, she cried out, *"Daddy, where are you?"* He intentionally did not answer her. She panicked and began to run. Then he carefully stepped in front of her so she would run into him. As she ran into his waiting arms, she exclaimed, *"O Daddy, I found you."*

This expresses the way the Lord relates to us. We often start to run without direction or purpose and the Lord places Himself in the very center of our path, so we also will run into Him. We are seeking and finding a God who has first sought after and then found us. If our heart interest is toward Him, we can trust Him to make Himself available to us.

The first confession of the Bride had been, *"My Beloved is mine."* At that time in her experience, she was diligently seeking after all that He was able to give her, which would make her comfortable and satisfied.

> **"Because of the savor of Your good ointments Your name *is as* ointment poured forth, therefore do the virgins love You."** Song of Solomon 1:3

She is saying, *"Because of all the things that I am receiving from you, I love You."* She is spiritually content, satisfied with all that has been provided and desires nothing further.

> **"As the apple tree among the trees of the wood, so *is* my Beloved among the sons. I sat down under His shadow with great delight, and His fruit *was* sweet to my taste."** Song of Solomon 2:3

A time came however, when all these *"things"* were removed, and she was completely alone in what seemed to be a place of spiritual darkness. All she was able to say was:

> **"By night on my bed I sought Him... but I found Him not."** Song of Solomon 3:1

In the darkness of this experience, none of her gifts would operate, nor could she *"feel"* the presence of the Lord; she felt that He had left her. Finally, as she struggled with these feelings, she turned and began to search for the Lord Himself.

> **"...I sought Him whom my soul loves...."** Song of Solomon 3:1

Previously, upon her bed, she had loudly proclaimed that she was desperately seeking Him, but had been unable to find Him. Now He is ready to test the sincerity of the declaration that she made (*By night on my bed I sought Him*), to see if she really meant it. Therefore, He came to her in the night season, after she had retired and knocked on the door of her heart, saying:

> **"...Open to Me, My sister, My love, My dove, My undefiled: for My head is filled with dew,** *and* **My locks with the drops of the night."** Song of Solomon 5:2

This reveals another spiritual principle. The Lord will deliberately come to us at a time when we are preoccupied with other things. He will do this when we least expect Him, to expose what really matters to us, and especially, to test the extravagant promises we express concerning our love and desire toward Him.

Notice that His head was filled with "*dew.*" The Lord had been seeking for fellowship elsewhere, but had not been able to find it. Therefore, He returned to her. We seldom realize the importance of our being able to discern His presence, and the value of our having the *spiritual sensitivity* and the *determined will* to respond to His invitation to fellowship.

> **"And I will give you the treasures of darkness, and hidden riches of secret places, that you may know that I, the Lord, which call** *you* **by your name,** *am* **the God of Israel."** Isaiah 45:3

> **"I will bless the Lord, who has given me counsel: my reins also instruct me in the night seasons."** Psalm 16:7

These "*night seasons*" are special times during which the Lord comes to knock on the door of our heart, desiring fellowship. This often happens during the night, especially at 3 AM, and reveals to us that He is a seeking God who searches for those who are willing to pay whatever price is required in order to respond to Him.

This "*importune*" knocking of the Lord on the door of our heart, seeking a response from us, will reveal what is really important to us. Unless we have dealt with our predisposition toward our personal comfort, and have determined to "*overcome*" any hindrance, we will make some excuse as to why we cannot respond, or we will try to delay our response until a more convenient time. We may say to the Lord, "*I will respond later, as I am very busy now.*" This indicates that something else is more important to us than the Lord Himself. Whatever it may be, it should be considered as being an idol.

We may have criticized the children of Israel for their idols, not realizing that we also may have our own. An "*idol*" is anything that becomes a substitute, or takes the place of the Lord in our spiritual experience. When the Lord reveals Himself to us, He expects a response. If we respond, "*Yes, Lord, but...*" and put Him off for some reason, that object or reason becomes as an idol which stands between the Lord and us.

When the Lord knocked on the *heart door* of His Bride and said, "*Open to Me,*" she offered a reasonable excuse. So also, when the Lord comes to knock on the door of our heart, we must make a choice. The Lord may come on a cold night and knock, while we are warm and comfortable in our bed. We can decide to respond in obedience, delay our response with an excuse, or fail to respond at all.

If we have made Jesus our "*Lord,*" from that time onward we have *no rights.* No matter how valid our reasons for not responding may be, His desire for our attention or fellowship must rise above and be more important than the right to our own personal comfort and privacy. Too easily, we become busy or preoccupied with many things, and then we use these as an excuse for our unresponsiveness to His desire for our time.

It is not only the carnal or sinful things that keep us from responding to the manifestation of His presence; it may be things that are good, legitimate, and necessary. Everything else must become secondary to our times of communion and fellowship with Jesus if we value His presence in our daily pattern of life.

If we intend to climb the stairs into the realm of intimacy and identity with Jesus in His eternal purposes, we must learn to discern (*notice*) His presence and then promptly respond to His desire to manifest Himself to us, regardless of our preoccupation. She said to the Lord:

"I have put off my coat; how shall I put it on? I have washed my feet; how shall I defile them?" Song of Solomon 5:3

Here, the Lord of Glory was knocking on the door of the heart of His Bride, seeking her attention. He was asking her to turn aside from whatever she was doing at that moment and separate herself to Him for whatever time He may have desired. She did not respond in *"prompt obedience"* to His knocking, because to do so would have been inconvenient to her personal comfort. It would have required her to get out of her warm, comfortable bed. Her excuse was hardly comparable to the vast possibilities that would have been made available to her, had she obeyed.

During the time in which she lived, houses had dirt floors, and open sandals were worn. Therefore, before she could retire for the night, she had to wash her feet. She was saying, *"If I get out of bed to open the door, I will have to walk through the dirt, and it will be necessary for me to again wash my feet. I just do not feel like doing this and besides, I am very tired."* She was not willing to inconvenience her flesh. Her comfort was more important to her than His presence.

Obedience to the Lord involves taking up a cross. Our natural being will always react to this.

"For the flesh lusts against the Spirit, and the Spirit against the flesh: and these are contrary the one to the other: so that you cannot do the things that you would." Galatians 5:17

The inconveniences that we must endure, or overcome, in being obedient to the Lord, are a very small price to pay in order to climb the stairs (*rise above all earthly desires*) and experience a rewarding time of communion with Jesus in His chambers.

We must take up our cross and allow all fleshly desires (*the personal comforts of our self-life*) to die upon it, whatever the cost may be. By a determined act of will, our "*spirit*" should continually be "*poised*" upward toward the Lord. We must develop and then maintain, a "*quality of spirit*" that is both perceptive (*sensitive*) and receptive (*willing*) to hear His voice. Then, when He knocks upon the door of our spirit, we will be able to respond quickly and invite Him to come within.

The excuse the Bride gave was both legitimate and true. Nevertheless, the Bridegroom was grieved due to the delay in her response, and He left. The "*way of entrance*" (*door*) that leads to the place of ascent had been placed in her path, but she failed to respond and enter. The Lord even knocked to help guide her to the place of entrance to the stairs. He made it as easy as He could for her to ascend into the place that He had prepared for her.

Because her "*temporary*" personal comfort was affected, she did not obey. Therefore, she lost an "*eternal*" reward. The eternal gains that result from our "*willing obedience*" are far greater in value than any temporal comfort that we may lose. By considering the consequences of her failure, we will be able to understand that obedience to our Lord's promptings is far more important than we may have realized.

Our responding to the Lord's knock upon the door of our spirit will open to us a realm of cooperative communion and experience with Him, beyond anything we could anticipate.

"If you be willing and obedient, you shall eat the good of the land." Isaiah 1:19

153

Chapter 15

DISTINCTIONS THAT MAKE A DIFFERENCE

"There are threescore queens... My dove, My undefiled is *but* **one...."** Song of Solomon 6:8, 9

The certainty that all Christians experience the *"abiding presence"* of the Holy Spirit is *absolute.*

Apart from receiving Jesus as our personal Savior, there are no conditions to meet. For those who are redeemed, the indwelling presence of the Holy Spirit is a reality that can be depended upon. The Holy Spirit is always faithful in His ministry of maintaining our redemption and making Jesus known to us, and, He ever seeks to make Jesus personally real within us.

However, our experiencing the manifest presence of Jesus is *conditional.*

To have the *ability* to recognize His manifest presence when He comes and knocks on the door of our spirit, and the *capability* to rightly respond when He does, is dependent upon the development of our *"spiritual sensitivity,"* and the *"set of our spirit"* being toward Him.

This means we must prayerfully keep our spirit *"poised upward"* (*in anticipation*) toward Jesus, so we will be able to recognize His presence when He comes to make known His desire for fellowship with us. As our love for Jesus grows, we will find ourselves expectantly looking forward to these visitations of His *manifest* presence. This requires learning how to open the "*door of entrance*" into our spirit when the Lord comes to visit with us.

> **"Therefore if any man** *be* **in Christ,** *he is* **a new creature: old things are passed away; behold, all things are become new. And all things** *are* **of God, who has reconciled us to Himself by Jesus Christ....."** II Corinthians 5:17-18

In our new birth, we are spiritually *reborn* and become a "*new creation*." Just as our natural senses gradually mature as we grow, our newly created spiritual senses must be progressively developed.

> **"...There is a natural body, and there is a spiritual body."** I Corinthians 15:44

It is through these inner spiritual senses within our spiritual being that we perceive, or recognize the manifest presence of the Lord. "*Behold, I stand at the door, and knock*" (*Revelation 3:20*).

Those who truly desire the Lord's friendship will "*quickly respond*" to the manifestation of His presence and "*invite*" Him to come within the "*room*" of their spiritual being. This "*room*" is an area deep within our spirit where we commune with the Lord. It is a "*set apart*" place where Jesus is alone with us, and where we are alone with Him. As we expectantly invite Him to come within our spirit to sup with us, He will guide us to the stairs that lead upward to "*His chambers,*" where we sup in communion with Him in His manifest presence.

> **"That I may cause those that love Me to inherit substance; and I will fill their treasures."** Proverbs 8:21

Jesus longs for us to desire to know Him as a person, rather than to know Him only for what He provides. As we partake of His life, we become one with Him. Now, we are ready to go into the vineyards with Him.

The Heavenly Bridegroom attempted to visit His Bride at a time that was inconvenient for her; therefore, she failed to respond. Disappointed, He departed because of her reluctance to open "*the door of her spirit*" to fellowship with Him. But, all was not lost. Instead, He allowed her to recognize the essential difference that existed between the "*gifts and blessings*" that He left behind for her to find, and the tremendous value of His "*manifest presence.*"

During the time in which the Bride lived, the latch on the door of entrance into her home was located on the inside of the door. It could only be unlatched by reaching through a small hole in the door and unlocking it from within. This provided a limited means of privacy, security, and protection.

Jesus so intensely desired to be with His Bride that He reached toward the latch, through this opening in the door, but He did not open it. The "*door of entrance*" to our spiritual chamber is always within our control and may be opened only by us. This action of Jesus reaching toward the Bride deeply stirred her. Later, she testified concerning this:

> **"My Beloved put in His hand by the hole** *of the door*, **and my bowels** (*the inner depths of her being*) **were moved for Him."** Song of Solomon 5:4 (comment added)

The Lord will never invade or violate our privacy. We must open the door; He never will. This principle is established in Scripture. He will knock and then stand there, waiting for us to open the door; but He will leave if we do not respond.

> **"I rose up to open to my Beloved; and my hands dropped** *with* **myrrh, and my fingers** *with* **sweet smelling myrrh, upon the handles of the lock. I opened to my Beloved; but my Beloved had withdrawn Himself, and was gone: my soul failed when He spoke: I sought Him, but I could not find Him; I called Him, but He gave me no answer."** Song of Solomon 5:5-6

As He departed, He left a *"handful"* of blessings for her. When she touched the lock, this tangible anointing came onto her hands, *"my hands dropped with myrrh, and my fingers with sweet smelling myrrh."* Previously, she would have been content to have these, apart from Him; but now, she panicked and longed for the personal presence of the Bridegroom Himself.

When she noticed His hand reaching toward the latch as an expression of His desire to be with her, she (*finally*) responded and opened the door to Him. But because of the delay in her response, He had reluctantly withdrawn His *"manifest presence"* from the door of entrance to the chamber within her spirit. However, the anointing, or, the result of His presence, had remained upon the lock.

Many are not able to differentiate between these two aspects of His presence.

The first aspect of His presence is general, and relates to His sovereignty.

> **"...Do not I fill heaven and earth? says the Lord."**
> Jeremiah 23:24

This is the *"power"* of His presence that fills the heavens and the earth and is referred to as His *"omnipresence."*

The second aspect of His presence is specific, and relates to His person. This is the coming of Jesus to us as a person having intellect, will, and emotions, who desires to personally *"share Himself with us."* This speaks of a *"conditional"* visitation and is referred to as His *"manifest presence."*

> **"...He stands behind our wall, He looks forth at the windows, showing Himself through the lattice."**
> Song of Solomon 2:9

Jesus expresses in the Gospel of John, the conditions that will allow Him to personally manifest Himself to us.

"He that has My commandments, and keeps them, he it is that loves Me: and he that loves Me shall be loved of My Father, and I will love him, and will manifest Myself to him.

"Judas says to Him, not Iscariot, Lord, how is it that You will manifest Yourself to us, and not to the world? Jesus answered and said to him, If a man love Me, he will keep My words: and My Father will love him, and We will come to him, and make Our abode with him."
John 14:21-23

The experience of her failure to respond to the attempted visit of the Bridegroom became a very important "*step*" for the Bride in learning the "*secret*" (*a prompt response to His desire to be with her*) that will lead to the place of ascent into His chambers. This time, she missed her opportunity to respond to the manifest presence of the Lord. But she learned through her disobedience that she urgently needed to develop an inner spiritual sensitivity, so she could hear Him knocking upon the "*door*" of her chamber.

She also learned the importance of quickly responding to His approach, regardless of her present circumstances.

"I love them that love Me; and those that seek Me early (*without delay*) shall find Me." Proverbs 8:17 (comment added)

Previously, the Bride had picturesquely described a characteristic of the Bridegroom, His hesitation to reveal Himself because of His sensitivity to being rejected. She had said:

"My Beloved is like a roe or a young hart...."
Song of Solomon 2:9

She recognized that His manifest presence was delicate and could be easily grieved. Thus, she should have known that He would leave when she delayed in responding to Him. We can learn from her mistake so we do not become the cause of another disappointment to the Lord. We must be diligent in seeking to become more spiritually perceptive, enabling us to rightly discern His presence.

We need to be attentive in *"listening"* for His knock and promptly turn aside from whatever we may be doing, when He comes to reveal Himself to us. Then, in anticipation, we can invite Him to come within the *"chamber"* of our spirit.

After her failure to respond promptly to His visitation, the Bride made a second mistake. Instead of asking for His forgiveness, and then waiting for Him to come again, she returned to her old ways, seeking others for advice concerning the loss of His presence.

> **"The watchmen that went about the city found me, they smote me, they wounded me; the keepers of the walls took away my veil from me."** Song of Solomon 5:7

Again, the ministry turned on her because of her disobedience. They did not understand the *"inner workings"* that were taking place at this particular time to bring about the changes that would enable her to become more sensitive and responsive to His seeking presence.

> **"For we are His workmanship, created in Christ Jesus to good works, which God has before ordained that we should walk in them."** Ephesians 2:10

Unseen to these watchmen, the Lord was diligently at work, deep within her. He was enlarging her desire and capacity to maintain an attitude of *"expectancy"* concerning His visits to her. Along with this, He was creating within her the ability to better respond and move with Him in the outworking of His purposes when He came to her in His manifest presence. These watchmen could see only the surface problem, not the true inner need that was disturbing her. Therefore, they made her condition worse. There are times when the Lord alone can help us through difficult circumstances.

The Lord left her in this condition until He brought about the necessary changes within her. This time, her visit to the watchmen had a different outcome. Her heart had been captivated by the Lord, and she was earnestly searching for Him, rather than frantically seeking for His blessings, as in the past. Therefore, she recognized that the Lord was allowing her to be "*chastened*" through the ministry, that she might be inwardly changed.

"For whom the Lord loves He chastens...." Hebrews 12:6

Because she now understands that the Lord works "*all things together for good*," she is able to "*maintain*" a good attitude toward these watchmen. We too should be careful about giving expression to our feelings, concerning difficult situations in which we find ourselves, especially when we know that others may not understand. If we do express our need to them, our spirit may be damaged as a result of their negative response or reaction. It is exceedingly important that we discipline ourselves in order to "*maintain*" the sensitivity of our spirit to His presence.

After this experience with the watchmen, the Bride turned to those who should have been seeking Him with her, and said to them:

"I charge you, O Daughters of Jerusalem, if you find my Beloved, that you tell Him, that I *am* sick of love."
Song of Solomon 5:8

There are two different categories of Christians within the Church: the Bride, and the Daughters of Jerusalem.

The "*Bride*" is identified as being "*The Church within the Church*." The Bride first seeks and relates to the Lord, and then through Him, to others. The "*visible Church*" (*the Daughters of Jerusalem*), first relates to others within the Church, and through them, to the Lord. This is clearly demonstrated in the Song of Solomon. The Bride sees the Lord (*my Dove*); the Daughters only see the Bride.

"My dove, My undefiled is *but* one; she *is* the *only* one of her mother, she *is* the *choice* one of her that bore her.

The Daughters saw her, and blessed her...."
Song of Solomon 6:9-10

The Bride has captured the singular attention and interest of the Bridegroom and says to Him:

"Tell me, O You whom my soul loves, where You feed, where You make *Your flock* **to rest at noon: for why should I be as one that turns aside by the flocks of Your companions?"** Song of Solomon 1:7

She is no longer content to simply enjoy all the blessings of salvation, or with having a part in the program of the Church. She is reaching beyond this to the Lord Himself, and will only be satisfied with a personal relationship with Him.

The second group, the *"Daughters of Jerusalem,"* is saved and has some understanding of the things of God. They attend Church and become involved, but they are satisfied with being saved, healed, and blessed. Therefore, they say to the Bride:

"What *is* **your Beloved more than** *another* **beloved...?"**
Song of Solomon 5:9

They are saying, *"We have gone as far as we are willing to go; we will stay here. Besides, we do not see why we should go through all those dealings, like you do."*

The Bride was seeking the Lord because He had withdrawn His *"manifest presence"* from her. She could no longer be satisfied with just hearing a sermon and fellowshipping with those within the Church, as the Daughters of Jerusalem were doing. Therefore, as she desperately searched for the Lord of the program, she spoke to the *"Church visible,"* portrayed as being the *"Daughters of Jerusalem,"* and said:

"I charge you, O Daughters of Jerusalem, if you find my Beloved, that you tell Him, that I *am* **sick of love."**
Song of Solomon 5:8

The Daughters of Jerusalem (*Church visible*) answered her and said:

"What *is* your Beloved more than *another* beloved, O you fairest among women? what *is* your Beloved more than *another* beloved, that you do so charge us?"
Song of Solomon 5:9

They saw only the benefits of being a Christian. To them, going to Church represented an obligation, a duty fulfilled. Also, it provided them with a time for social fellowship and activities. The thought of entering His chambers for fellowship and communion with Jesus Himself was far from their minds or their interest. They could only say to the Bride:

"What is He more than a good job, a nice home, or security? What is He more than all of the good things we have? We are satisfied and content. We are the Daughters of Jerusalem (saved), and it is enough. Do not bother us with your seeking of the Lord; you are trying to be too spiritual."

They were as the Laodicean Church, of whom the Lord said:

"Because you say, I am rich, and increased with goods, and have need of nothing; and know not that you are wretched, and miserable, and poor, and blind, and naked." Revelation 3:17

But something had happened within the heart of the Bride. She had been in the garden alone with Jesus and experienced the joy and satisfaction of communion with Him. Now she longed for a continuing experience of His personal presence and friendship and felt incomplete when she was apart from Him. When the Daughters of Jerusalem said to her, *"What is He more than another,"* she did not tell them about all the blessings she had received from Him. Rather, she began to extol the Bridegroom Himself.

"My Beloved *is* white and ruddy, the chiefest among ten thousand. His head *is as* the most fine gold, His locks *are* bushy, *and* black as a raven. His eyes *are as the*

163

eyes **of doves by the rivers of waters, washed with milk,** *and* **fitly set. His cheeks** *are* **as a bed of spices,** *as* **sweet flowers: His lips** *like* **lilies, dropping sweet smelling myrrh. His hands** *are* **as gold rings set with the beryl: His belly** *is* **as bright ivory overlaid** *with* **sapphires. His legs** *are* **as pillars of marble, set upon sockets of fine gold: His countenance** *is* **as Lebanon, excellent as the cedars. His mouth** *is* **most sweet: yea, He** *is* **altogether lovely. This** *is* **my Beloved, and this** *is* **my Friend, O Daughters of Jerusalem.**" Song of Solomon 5:10-16

Because she had been spending time alone with her Beloved, the Lord Jesus, she was able to give an intimate description of Him. She could clearly describe His personality, because she had a single eye toward Him. She knew Him as an intimate Friend, and could give clear, authoritative expression to His beauty and desirability.

The Daughters of Jerusalem had said:

> "...**What** *is* **your Beloved more than** *another* **beloved, that you do so charge us?**" Song of Solomon 5:9

Due to her personal knowledge and relationship with Him, the Bride, with heart authority, exalted the Lord Jesus, and set Him forth as the answer to the inner cry of every heart. This brought a response from the Daughters of Jerusalem, which is so needed in our day of special gimmicks, rock-style music, and programs that are being used in an attempt to build up the Church.

> "**Where is your Beloved gone, O you fairest among women? where is your Beloved turned aside? that we may seek Him with you?**" Song of Solomon 6:1

Their spirit had been stirred by the testimony that flowed as a river from the inner depths of the Bride as she gave expression to her love for Him. She set forth the Lord Himself in evident view for the Daughters of Jerusalem to behold. In Acts 1:8 the Lord said: "*But you shall receive power, after that the Holy Ghost is come upon you: and you shall be witnesses to Me....*"

We ourselves are this witness. As we express our love to Him in the intimacy of His presence, His beauty is reflected through us for others to behold.

The enemy of our spiritual life continually seeks to turn us aside from seeking the Lord for Himself, and will attempt to tell us: "*It is selfish to endeavor to become spiritual, or to spend time waiting on the Lord. Rather, go out and do something for someone else.*" We can get so busy working for the Lord that we will have no time to prepare ourselves to work with Him. We cannot give what we do not have. Thus, our active personal relationship with Jesus will become a threat to the enemy of our spirituality.

The enemy knows the power that can flow through the life of the one who has been alone with the Lord in His chambers. He knows the heart cry of those who eagerly seek more, after they "*witness*" the beauty of Jesus being expressed through the life of His Bride.

"Where is your Beloved gone... **that we may seek Him with you."** Song of Solomon 6:1

As we lift our spirit in adoration toward Him, we will fall so completely in love with Jesus and become so like Him, that it will be He that is seen, rather than us. Then, wherever we go, His presence abiding in us will penetrate through every hindering bondage and fear within those who are witnessing the result of His life being resident in our life experience. This will bring others to a knowledge of Jesus Christ.

"For many are called, but few *are* **chosen."** Matthew 22:14

The "*many*" refers to the Daughters of Jerusalem. The "*few*" refers to the Bride. Another way to say this is: The Daughters of Jerusalem are "*called,*" but the Bride is being "*chosen*" from among them, because she has become willing to come apart and seek Him.

"There are threescore queens... My dove, My undefiled is *but* **one...."** Song of Solomon 6:8-9

Here again, two different categories are expressed: the called, and the chosen. The "*called*" includes all Christians. The "*chosen*" refers to those who have pressed on to know the Lord Himself. These chosen ones have discovered *the secret of the stairs* and have begun their upward climb into His chambers, to be with Him.

The Lord is calling a Bride out from among those who still are saying, "*I have gone to bed; how shall I get up?*" These Daughters of Jerusalem know the voice of the Lord to a degree, but they are not committed. They have a limited involvement in the Church and are willing to go only so far. They draw a line, refusing to go further. They say, "*I will not become one of those fanatics.*" They know there is a price to pay in order to enter His chambers; but they are not willing to pay it.

> **"...The Daughters saw her, and blessed her...."**
> Song of Solomon 6:9

They realize that the Bride has something they do not have. They have enough spiritual capacity to recognize the Bride, and enough spiritual sense to know they should bless her. They can only see the Lord through the description that the Bride willingly shares with them, when she, with a glow within her being, says to them, "*This is my Beloved, and this is my Friend, O Daughters of Jerusalem*" (Song of Solomon 5:16).

How much better it is to arise from our bed of indifference (*I have gone to bed, how shall I get up?*) and respond to His knocking on the door of our heart. As we then allow Him to guide us upward on the stairs to His chambers, we will come to intimately know Him. Then in His manifested presence, share together with Him in the outworking of His purposes. Now, He can say to us:

> **"Come, My beloved, let us go forth into the field; let us lodge in the villages. Let us get up early to the vineyards; let us see if the vine flourish,** *whether* **the tender grape**

appear, *and* **the pomegranates bud forth: there will I give you My loves."** Song of Solomon 7:11-12

"There will I give you My loves." Now, we, as His Bride, can respond, knowing that we have found that for which we had been searching, our Bridegroom, the Lord Jesus Christ.

Chapter 16

SATISFACTION AND
RESPONSIBILITY
IN ATTAINMENT

"I *am* **my Beloved's, and His desire** *is* **toward me."**
Song of Solomon 7:10

This is the third and final confession of the Bride. It reveals the extent of the complete change that has taken place. She has come to the place in her experience where she no longer needs to make demands on the Lord in order to find satisfaction. Rather, she has made herself totally available to Him for His purposes, as her life has merged into His life. Her *self-seeking* has been dealt with and is no longer a hindrance to their times of intimacy in the outworking of His purposes, both in and through her.

Finally, the Lord can expect a prompt and favorable response from His Bride, whenever He knocks on the door of her heart. He can invite her to come apart from her activities to be with Him, knowing that this is also her desire. As they walked through the vineyards together, the Bride became aware of a need:

> **"We have a little sister, and she has no breasts: what shall we do for our sister in the day when she shall be spoken for?"** Song of Solomon 8:8

She may now approach Jesus at any time to request His wisdom in behalf of the one for whom she is burdened; and with confidence she can expect a prompt response from Him, knowing that this is also His desire. In anticipation, she quietly waits until He responds with concern for the burden she feels.

The Lord quickly responded to her question, *"What shall we do?"* He offered to work with His Bride (*we will ...*) to bring about the necessary correction.

> **"If she *be* a wall, we will build upon her a palace of silver: and if she *be* a door, we will enclose her in boards of cedar."** Song of Solomon 8:9

His answer was practical and dealt with the root of the problem, her spiritual immaturity, rather than the obvious, *"she has no breasts."* It set forth the course of action that should be taken concerning the need of this spiritually immature *"little sister."*

First, the Lord exposed her deficiency in foundational truth; she was unstable, like a *"swinging door."* This resulted in her lack of spiritual growth (*she did not have breasts*). Then He, through the *"spirit of knowledge and wisdom,"* revealed the way to effectively bring about the needed correction, *"We will enclose her in boards of cedar."*

His solution involves correcting this little sister's instability through teaching and quiet meditation (*learning to spend quality time, waiting on the Lord*). *"Teaching"* will enable her to receive the Word as spiritual *substance* and *life*, and then through *"demonstration"* (*example*), show her how to receive spiritual strength as she waits upon the Lord. Now, she will be protected from temptation (*enclosed in boards of cedar*) while the foundation for her faith is being established as a *"wall"* (*strong enough to help others*).

After this is accomplished, a further work will be needed. A *"habitation"* for His presence (*a palace of silver*) is to be built upon the foundation that is being established. Our salvation experience is merely the *"beginning"* of the complete work that the Lord desires to do within each of us.

"Now therefore you are no more strangers and foreigners, but fellow citizens with the saints, and of the household of God; And are built upon the foundation of the apostles and prophets, Jesus Christ Himself being the chief corner *stone*; In whom all the building fitly framed together grows to a holy temple in the Lord: In whom you also are built together for a habitation of God through the Spirit." Ephesians 2:19-22

The *vision* of the Bridegroom (*His desire for an active, cooperative relationship with His Bride*), along with the *burden* of the Bride, are merged into a single concern for this little sister who is spiritually immature. While Jesus ministers His love to the Bride, together they will minister their love to this little sister, as she matures. No longer does the Bride need to say:

"...my mother's children were angry with me; they made me the keeper of the vineyards...." Song of Solomon 1:6

She has *learned* the secret of entrance into His chambers and has *experienced* the joy of working "*with*" the Lord, rather than "*for*" Him. The *frustration* of trying to please others, along with the *pressure* of duty, is gone. In their place is the deep inner peace and fulfillment that results from working together.

"...there will I give you My loves." Song of Solomon 7:12

The Lord revealed the spiritual principle that relates to this need: "*If she be a wall, we will build;*" or, "*If she be a door, we will enclose.*" Then He waited for the Bride to determine which of these, a "*door*" or a "*wall*," expressed the present spiritual condition and need of this young Christian. The Lord is beginning to introduce His Bride to a place of spiritual responsibility in His Kingdom.

The first possibility, "*If she be a wall,*" speaks of the spiritual stability that results from our understanding the foundational doctrines upon which we stand. As these basic principles are established within our spirit, the Lord will then be able to build upon this foundation.

> **"Therefore whosoever hears these sayings of Mine, and does them, I will liken him to a wise man, which built his house upon a rock: And the rain descended, and the floods came, and the winds blew, and beat upon that house; and it fell not: for it was founded upon a rock. And every one that hears these sayings of Mine, and does them not, shall be likened to a foolish man, which built his house upon the sand: And the rain descended, and the floods came, and the winds blew, and beat upon that house; and it fell: and great was the fall of it. And it came to pass, when Jesus had ended these sayings, the people were astonished at his doctrine: For he taught them as *one* having authority, and not as the scribes."** Matthew 7:24-29

The Lord speaks of what is to be built upon this foundation. This visible *"righteous witness"* relates to the quality of our spiritual experience and should appear to others as being a *"palace of silver"* (Song of Solomon 8:9).

This involves *"righteous deeds,"* or right living, in our daily pattern of life. The foundation upon which our spiritual growth is built is extremely important. Otherwise, the manifestation of our spiritual life will be faulty, and we may be viewed by others as being a *"shanty of lead,"* rather than a *"palace of silver."*

The second possibility, *"If she be a door,"* refers to spiritual instability. This confused state of being comes through a flawed understanding of our spiritual revelations and experiences. Such confusion would cause her to function like a door that is hung on double-swing hinges so it can open, first one way, and then suddenly swing the opposite way. This *"swinging door"* condition requires a constant vigilance and care, until a degree of stability can be developed in her spiritual experience. Therefore, the Lord said she was to be *"enclosed in boards of cedar."*

This speaks of our being submitted to pastoral protection, or the oversight of a mature Christian, until that which keeps us spiritually immature (*a swinging door*) has been revealed, dealt with, and corrected. We must dig down through and remove the *"rubble"* that hinders our spiritual growth, until we are established as being a *"wall."* This rubble may have accumulated due to prayers that were not answered as we anticipated, or from a prophetic word that did not lead to the expected results, thus leaving us confused and feeling that the Lord does not care about us. If we do not deal with these issues and remove this *"rubble,"* our spiritual vision may become cloudy.

The protection, guidance, and love that is extended to this little sister will encourage her, and give her time to discover and remove all mixture from her spiritual experience, until she can stand firmly on the solid *"Rock"* that is beneath. Only then will she be able to abide on this rock foundation, our Lord Jesus Christ.

The needs of this *"little sister"* were met because of the close relationship between the Bridegroom and the Bride. The Bride has come into an experience of direct communion with the Bridegroom and is willing to respond to His every desire, as when He said to her:

> **"Come, My beloved, let us go forth into the field...."**
> Song of Solomon 7:11

The Bridegroom is in direct communion with the Bride and is waiting to respond to her every desire, as when she said to Him, *"We have a little sister, what shall we do for her?"* This cooperative relationship between the Bridegroom and the Bride has gradually developed into a beautifully productive communion. Such needs as this can now be met, as, *together*, each contributes their part.

This came about as the result of an ongoing process in which the Bride has been gradually drawn by the Bridegroom, *step upon step*, into His chambers. He approached the Bride again and again, knocking upon the door of her heart, seeking entrance into her life. The Bride, through many lessons, including her failures and mistakes, has learned to recognize and respond to His presence.

Over a period of time, her obedience has resulted in an "*open door*" into her heart, through which the Lord might enter at will to invite His Bride to "*rise up and come away*" to share with Him in fellowship and also, to cooperate with Him in the outworking of His purposes.

This *open door* into the heart and life of His Bride, which was gained by the Lord's unceasing perseverance, has also benefited her. Now she may approach Him whenever she wishes to ask His counsel and help concerning the needs for which she has a burden.

The complete change in her is apparent, for we recall that in the beginning, she sought to possess the Bridegroom for her own satisfaction and said, "*He is mine*" (Song of Solomon 2:16). At that time, she was content with the things that He provided and willingly abode alone in His *shadow*, having no desire to personally experience His presence. However, this did not discourage the Lord; for He patiently led His Bride, step upon step, upward toward His chambers where she could "*sup*" with Him in His presence.

As a result of the spiritual "*substance*" that she received during these times of "*supping*" with the Bridegroom, she has come into a fully developed, cooperative relationship that holds special meaning and purpose both to her, and to the Lord. Of this fully developed relationship with the Lord, the Bride testifies:

> **"I** *am* **a wall, and my breasts like towers....**"
> Song of Solomon 8:10

Now, those who are as a "*little sister*" will be able to receive from her the spiritual nourishment they desperately need, so they also may grow into the same "*stature*" of spiritual maturity as she. Not only does she have this ability to feed others; she is also able to fulfill a desire that has been within the Lord, since He came to walk with Adam in the Garden of Eden.

When tested, Adam failed; but the Bride, through testing, has proven herself to be qualified. Therefore, her spiritual walk is now as stable as a *"wall,"* and the Lord with confidence may now say to His Bride:

> **"How beautiful are your feet with shoes, O prince's daughter...!"** Song of Solomon 7:1

He can come during the *"cool of the day"* (Genesis 3:8) and find her waiting in anticipation, ready to *"walk"* through the vineyards with Him, as they reach out to others who desire to be nurtured and brought to the level of spiritual maturity that she now enjoys.

> **"To him that overcomes will I grant to sit with Me in My throne, even as I also overcame, and am set down with My Father in His throne."** Revelation 3:21

It is necessary that we *"qualify"* before we can fully experience all that is included in being espoused to the Heavenly Bridegroom.

> **"Let us rejoice and be glad and give the glory to Him, for the marriage of the Lamb has come and His Bride has made herself ready. It was given to her to clothe herself in fine linen, bright and clean; for the fine linen is the righteous acts of the saints."** Revelation 19:7-8 NAS

This *"processing"* began when she, as one of the many Daughters of Jerusalem, began to see the Bridegroom with a *"single eye"* and said to Him, *"Draw me, we (all of me) will run after You"* (Song of Solomon 1:4). This touched His heart, and He responded and began to look toward her with a *"single eye."* She had gained His approbation, or favor.

Now, the Lord was stirred with desire to become active within her, to bring about the changes that led to her three progressive testimonies. Her *"response"* to His presence, along with her *"willing obedience"* to the circumstances that He placed in her path to provoke these changes, qualified her to enter each higher level of experience to become the Bride that He desired.

To better understand this *"conditional"* relationship, it is helpful to consider the spiritual condition of those who have not qualified to be His Bride. The distinction between the two is particularly evident as we compare the spiritual position, experience, and perspective of the Bride to that of the Daughters of Jerusalem.

The Bride has direct access to the Lord through her personal relationship with Him. She is able to give an intimate description of Him, and of the resultant blessings of her communion with Him. She expressed to the Daughters of Jerusalem a very detailed description of His person and His desirability. She could say from experience:

> **"His mouth *is* most sweet: yea, He *is* altogether lovely. This *is* my Beloved, and this *is* my Friend, O Daughters of Jerusalem."** Song of Solomon 5:16

The Daughters of Jerusalem have indirect access to the Lord through their relationship with the Bride. The only vision they have of the Lord is that which they receive through the Bride. They know Him only through the Bride.

> **"Where is your Beloved gone, O you fairest among women? where is your Beloved turned aside? that we may seek Him with you?"** Song of Solomon 6:1

The only description the Daughters are able to give is that of the Bride, from whom they draw their spiritual life.

> **"...The Daughters saw her, and blessed her; *yea,* the queens and the concubines, and they praised her."** Song of Solomon 6:9

The way in which the Bride sees the Lord, in contrast to the

Daughters' perception of Him, is the result of a very noticeable difference in their relationship to Him. The Bride is enjoying the personal presence of the Lord and is involved with Him in a ministry in the vineyards. She can speak directly to Him and express the burden of her heart. The Daughters of Jerusalem are mainly concerned with things of lesser importance and can only say to the Bride:

"What *is* your Beloved more than *another* beloved, O you fairest among women? what *is* your Beloved more than *another* beloved, that you do so charge us?"
Song of Solomon 5:9

Within each Christian fellowship are two representative groups that are similar, yet different from each other. There is a group much like these Daughters of Jerusalem; they see the Lord only through the lives of those who live so close to Him that, *as a mirror*, they reflect His person and presence. Just as the Daughters of Jerusalem were busy with other things, these nominal Christians are content with the memory of their past experiences. They receive their spiritual nourishment from those who are fully committed (*the Bride*). Because these Daughters (*nominal Christians*) affect her spiritual life and walk, the Bride has much to overcome.

The Daughters of Jerusalem said to the Bride, *"What is He more than another?"* Their testimony expressed the reality of their salvation, but it is evident that they had not grown beyond this point. They chose to live in comfort, as it pleased them. They did not make themselves available to be disciplined by the Lord as the Bride had. Rather, having spent their lifetime accumulating the riches of this world, they failed to purchase eternal treasures.

There is today an innumerable company of believers who sense that there is something more to life than all that they possess. They are *"searching"* for Jesus, and are *"catching"* His eye and interest. The Lord is calling these out from *"among"* the

Daughters to go through a time of preparation in order to become a part of His corporate Bride. He will soon call them to *"rise up and come away"* (Revelation 12:5). It is obvious that the Daughters of Jerusalem will be left behind, when this takes place.

We are making our decisions now concerning eternity. The time that we have been given here on earth in order to make these choices, is the most important time in all eternity.

"In my Father's house are many mansions...." John 14:2

This can be expressed in another way; *"There are many levels of spiritual attainment to which we can ascend by entering the Secret of the Stairs."* The *vertical* level to which we attain (*our spiritual growth*) will be determined by the cumulative result of our choices, decisions, and attitudes toward the things of God that we make during our life time. In heaven, this will become the *horizontal* level upon which we will expand and move, throughout eternity.

This is the importance of our understanding the *"secret"* of the stairs, which is known only by those who are spiritually perceptive. Each step on the stairs will bring us upward into a new level. In heaven, there is no suffering, no temptation, and no devil to try us. Therefore, as we ascend, our revelations and experiences will be tested and proven. If we are faithful in these testings, our being *"called"* by the Lord will lead us upward to the place where we will be *"chosen"* by Him to become His Bride.

We are to continue our upward climb on these stairs. Our time on earth is probationary to determine how high we will go. If we say, *"This is as far as I am going,"* then throughout all eternity, we will remain on that level, while others may have gone further. In eternity, it is too late for us to go higher. Therefore, Paul said:

"If by any means I might attain to the resurrection of the dead." Philippians 3:11

He is speaking of an *"out-resurrection"* from among the living dead, a resurrection from among the Daughters of Jerusalem, *"up"* into the Bride. Paul saw the difference in these groups and sought the higher level. Thus he said:

"I press toward the mark for the prize of the high calling of God in Christ Jesus." Philippians 3:14

The first confession of the Bride had been, *"My Beloved is mine"* (Song of Solomon 2:16). She felt that she possessed Him and was busy at work *"for"* Him; but she had no relationship *"with"* Him. Nevertheless, through many progressive dealings, she came to the place where she found that she could be satisfied only by being in His presence. Then her confession became, *"I am my Beloved's and my Beloved is mine"* (Song of Solomon 6:3). Once she had personally met Him, she placed Him first in her life.

The Lord began to escort her upward to yet another step. She was again led into the wilderness so she might experience becoming totally dependent upon Him. The daughters noticed the result of her time with Him in the wilderness and said:

"Who *is* this that comes up from the wilderness, leaning upon her Beloved...?" Song of Solomon 8:5

Now, the Bride is able to say, *"I am my Beloved's, and His desire is toward me"* (Song of Solomon 7:10). Jesus has become her all in all, and only now can He say to her, *"Come, My beloved, let us go forth into the field* (Song of Solomon 7:11).

The *"call"* of God is never simply to *"go;"* it includes the time during which we are first to *"come."* When the Lord called Moses to deliver His people from Egypt, He said to Moses, *"Come now therefore, and I will send you to Pharaoh"* (Exodus 3:10). The call to *"come"* included his time of preparation, so he could be *"sent"* with the enabling grace and giftings, to bring deliverance to the Lord's people. We cannot give what we do not have.

When Peter was called, Jesus said, *"Come you after Me, and I will make you to become fishers of men"* (Mark 1:17). If we are faithful in our coming to *"sup"* with Him, He will be faithful in sending us.

The Lord had said to His Bride, *"Let us go forth into the field."* This *"field"* speaks of our place of testimony and service. Her mother's children had forced the Bride to keep the vineyard. Now, the Lord Himself is leading her into the vineyard. No longer is she working for the Lord; rather, she is working in *"divine union"* with Him.

This is the reason for the *"secret"* concerning the stairs. The way of entrance and our ascent to His chambers is *"revealed"* only to those who seek Him with a *"single eye"* (*one thing have I desired*), and with heart sincerity pray, *"draw me."* This must be followed by a total commitment to a *"willing obedience"* that enables us to *"run after Him."*

> **"One thing have I desired of the Lord, that will I seek after; that I may dwell in the house of the Lord all the days of my life, to behold the beauty of the Lord, and to inquire in His temple. For in the time of trouble He shall hide me in His pavilion: in the secret of His tabernacle shall He hide me; He shall set me up upon a rock."** Psalm 27:4-5

Our ascent up the stairs will lead us into His chambers, where, as we commune with Jesus, He will take us yet further, as together we enter into the *"Secret of His Tabernacle."* Here, we will experience inexhaustible levels of revelation and understanding as our identity with Him as His Bride further unfolds. As we are seated together with Him in His throne, our identity and function as the visible expression of His life and ministry in His coming Kingdom, will begin to function in the outworking of His eternal purposes.

Because of this progression in purpose and goal, the Bride faces a greater measure of responsibility.

"...For to whomsoever much is given, of him shall be much required...." Luke 12:48

With privilege comes responsibility. The Lord places much responsibility on those whom He knows and can trust.

"Solomon had a vineyard at Baal-hamon; He let out the vineyard to keepers; every one for the fruit thereof was to bring a thousand *pieces* **of silver."** Song of Solomon 8:11

The Lord expects those who know Him and have an understanding of His ways, to bring forth a very fruitful harvest. From the fruit of their harvest, He expects to receive a thousand pieces of silver as His portion.

The Bride also has a vineyard, the Daughters of Jerusalem, for whom she is responsible.

"My vineyard, which *is* **mine,** *is* **before me: you O Solomon,** *must have* **a thousand, and those who keep the fruit thereof two hundred."** Song of Solomon 8:12

She is expected to provide Solomon with "*a thousand*" from her vineyard, while those who were dependent upon her are only required to supply "*two hundred*." More is required of her because He has personally worked with her in the vineyard.

As we spend time with the Lord in His chambers, our capacity is enlarged and we become capable of accomplishing much more, as we have direct access to His wisdom. Although greater responsibility is involved, the joy of communion with Him makes it all worthwhile.

If we are true to all that we have been taught and experienced, the day will come when we will hear with gladness:

"...Well done, good and faithful servant; you have been faithful over a few things, I will make you ruler

over many things: enter you into the joy of your lord."
Matthew 25:23

This will be a glorious day...

CONCLUSION

The purpose of the Lord in preserving the manuscript of the Song of Solomon to become a part of our Bible extends far beyond the knowledge which can be gleaned from it concerning Solomon seeking after the Shulamite. The Song of Solomon is best read in the King James Translation.

The message that lives within the pages of this book transcends time and reaches out to touch us, just as though we were this Shulamite. As we prayerfully meditate upon the Song of Solomon, we discover that this *"Bride to be"* is being patiently, yet persistently drawn into a relationship of intimacy with her Heavenly Bridegroom, our Lord Jesus.

First, she is delivered from her *self-centered* seeking. Then, she is separated from among the *Daughters of Jerusalem*. Finally, as she becomes dissatisfied with *all else*, and with a single eye, she longs for the personal presence of the Bridegroom.

In the same way, if we desire to become a part of His corporate Bride, we also will be *"processed"* by the Lord. We will be separated from all that is less than His best, and we will be drawn out from among the present day *"Daughters of Jerusalem."* Then, as His Bride, we will be seen coming up out of the wilderness of our day, *"leaning"* upon our Beloved in total dependence upon Him.

This *"processing"* is costly and will require much from each of us who desire to become a part of His corporate Bride that is yet being prepared, of whom the Scripture says:

> **"Blessed** *are* **they which are called to the marriage supper of the Lamb....**" Revelation 19:9

The love relationship that developed between the Bridegroom and the one who has captivated His heart, is laid out before us within the pages of this book, *The Secret of the Stairs*. As we find our way upward on the *"stairs"* and into His *"chambers,"* we will experience an inner satisfaction and fulfillment that far transcends anything that the world may offer.

The *"potential"* to experience this same beautiful love relationship with the Lord is resident within each of us. This time of preparation begins with our becoming willing to receive correction concerning all *self-centeredness*, along with our desire for self-fulfillment and satisfaction. Progressively, we will be enabled to discover the *"secrets"* that will set us free as we move upward with Him, becoming so transparent that His life will be seen through our lives.

To those who have been *"touched"* by the searching love of the Heavenly Bridegroom, and who have a *"compelling desire"* to intimately know Him, the spiritual truths and principles that are revealed within the pages of this book, *The Secret of the Stairs*, will become brightly illuminated. You will be given the *"key"* to unlock the door of entrance into the progressive *"workings"* which will *"prepare"* you to be presented to Jesus, as His Bride made ready for *"that day."*

If this is the desire of your heart, and if you have not yet found the way upward on the stairs that lead to His chambers, then prayerfully re-read the pages of this book, placing yourself in the *"shoes"* of the *"Bride"* who lives within the Song of Solomon; and then, walk with her, step by step, through all that brought her into the chambers of the Heavenly Bridegroom.

To all others, the pages of this book will be but a record of Solomon seeking after the Shulamite.

As you pray, *"draw me,"* and respond, you will gain much spiritual understanding and insight. You will discover, with a thankful heart, that the experiences of the Bride are being relived within your life.

As you experience intimate communion with the Heavenly Bridegroom, our Lord Jesus, He in turn, will share with you His burden for mankind. Then as you lean upon Him, together, you will walk into all that He intends, now, and in the ages to come.

And, He will reveal to you the fullness of His love, without end...

Books by Wade E. Taylor

THE SECRET OF THE STAIRS

The *"The Secret of the Stairs"* reveals the progressive steps that lead to our coming into an intimate, personal relationship with the Lord Jesus. It begins with our self-centeredness, and ends with our being the Bride that our Lord desires.

WATERSPOUTS OF GLORY

The *"Waterspouts of Glory"* relates to our *"being made ready"* to have a part in the end-time revelation of the glory of our Lord. It expresses the principles and the method by which we come into a committed life and overcome.

UNLOCKING THE MYSTERIES OF THE KINGDOM

The *"Unlocking the Mysteries of the Kingdom"* speaks of our experiencing a cooperative relationship with our Lord in the outworking of His *"end-time"* purposes, for which He is drawing us to Himself.

BEING MADE READY
A DAILY DEVOTIONAL

The *"Being Made Ready A Daily Devotional"* calls us to come up. The message of the kingdom is meant to be a present reality in our lives. Our Lord Jesus is, at this present time, preparing a people who are hearing and responding–in heart obedience to Him.

Deeper Life Teaching
CD Albums by Wade E. Taylor
There are 6 CD's in each set.

Developing a Devotional Life – Our Lord is a seeking God, Who is very desirous for our fellowship. He will, as we seek to better know Him, create within us a hunger that will lead us into His manifest presence that we might intimately know, and personally sup with Him.

Messages for Our Times – A collection of teachings given by Wade Taylor. These timely, selected teachings are intended to present the anointed Word as spiritual food for those who desire to go further in their relationship with the Lord, and to be prepared to participate with Him in the outworking of His end-time purposes.

Kingdom Progression – There is a present call from the Lord to "come up" into a higher realm of understanding and relationship to the Lord. We are living in the final hours of our being made ready for our part in this time of transition into the Millennial Kingdom.

Single teaching CD's and DVD's are also available.

To Order
books, teaching CD and DVD sets, or single teaching CD's and DVD's by Wade E. Taylor

Please call, write, or visit our website

Online Orders
www.wadetaylorpublications.org

Phone
1-800-349-0340

Email
orders@wadetaylorpublications.org

Write To
wtp@wadetaylorpublications.org

CPSIA information can be obtained
at www.ICGtesting.com
Printed in the USA
LVHW080727160421
684558LV00006B/57

9 780974 769035